New Studies in the Philosophy of John Dewey

New Studies in the Philosophy of John Dewey

edited by Steven M. Cahn

Published for The University of Vermont by
The University Press of New England
Hanover, New Hampshire, 1977

Publication of this book has been assisted by generous
support from The John Dewey Foundation.

The University Press
of New England

Sponsoring Institutions
Brandeis University
Clark University
Dartmouth College
The University of New Hampshire
The University of Rhode Island
The University of Vermont

Contents

Introduction

STEVEN M. CAHN

The six essays that comprise this volume were originally delivered as lectures at The University of Vermont
during April and May 1975. Each of the lecturers was
asked to discuss the relevance of John Dewey's thought
to contemporary work in one specific area of philosophy. Although most of the lectures have been slightly
modified to meet demands of the written word as well
as points raised in discussion, in substance this collec-
tion is composed of the talks as we heard them.

It is appropriate that these lectures were given at The
University of Vermont, for John Dewey was at heart
a Vermonter. He was born in Burlington in 1859,
attended elementary and secondary schools there, was
graduated from The University of Vermont, and later
taught high school in Charlotte. When on the occasion
of his ninetieth birthday he spoke at a celebration in his
honor at his alma mater, he emphasized how strongly
his experiences as a Vermont youth had influenced his
intellectual development.

Ironically, Dewey, so long the dominant force on the American philosophical scene, is now, less than twenty-five years after his death, no longer much studied or even discussed. Indeed, many philosophers today are surprised to learn of the eminent position he was accorded by his contemporaries throughout the world. In the late 1930's, when the first volume in Paul Arthur Schilpp's *The Library of Living Philosophers* appeared, its subject was not, as we now might suppose, Bertrand Russell or G. E. Moore or Alfred North Whitehead or George Santayana. It was John Dewey, and this choice is clearly justified by one of Whitehead's remarks in the volume: "We are living in the midst of the period subject to Dewey's influence." Whitehead went on to stress the significance of Dewey's philosophical thought for the development of American civilization, and he classed Dewey with philosophers whom he viewed as having performed an analogous role in their own societies—Augustine, Aquinas, Descartes, and Locke.

Why is Dewey at present a comparatively neglected figure? The answer does not lie, as has been suggested, in difficulties posed by the thickets of his prose, for stylistic barriers have not prevented other profound thinkers from maintaining their rightful places in the philosophical pantheon. Rather, as I see it, the strong British influence on the development of post-World War II American philosophy led many to overemphasize the virtues of what appeared to be pure philosophical analysis untarnished by any connections with normative concerns. The so-called "revolution in philosophy" prided itself on the very limitations of its enterprise. Consider, for example, these words by Gilbert Ryle at the beginning of an essay he wrote entitled "Teaching and Training": "I have no teaching tricks or pedagogic maxims to impart to you, and I should not impart them to you if I had any." Anyone who shares this outlook will have little sympathy for the author of *The School and Society, The Child and the Curriculum*, and *Democracy and Education*. Dewey, after all, believed that one of philosophy's crucial tasks is "the search for values to be secured and shared by all," and that is precisely the search eschewed by the makers of the British philosophical revolution.

But the ideological fervor of that revolution has now passed, and the last decade has witnessed a major revival of interest in central questions of personal morality and public policy. Perhaps then the time is right for a renewal of interest in Dewey's philosophy and its attempt "to interpret the conclusions of science with respect to their consequences for our beliefs about purposes and values in all phases of life."

The contributors to this volume have set out to discuss those aspects of Dewey's thought most pertinent to present-day philosophical concerns. The essays, however, are not intended to be mere reverential summaries of Dewey's views. On the contrary, they are critical essays that bring to the fore the author's agreements and disagreements with Dewey's positions. The aim has been to take seriously what Dewey had to say and to subject it to the most careful scrutiny. That is precisely the way one ought to pay tribute to a great philosopher.

The publication of this work coincides with the Bicentennial celebration in the United States. I find this coincidence a happy one, for no philosopher better understood the spirit of our country than John Dewey, and none expressed its ideals more profoundly. Dewey was, in Sidney Hook's words, "the philosopher of American democracy," and his writings continue to speak directly to those who share the vision of America's founders and who wish to make of that vision a reality.

The Contributors

Steven M. Cahn is Professor of Philosophy and Chairman of the Department at The University of Vermont. Previously he taught at Dartmouth College, Vassar College, The University of Rochester, and New York University. He has authored or edited six other books, including *Fate, Logic, and Time* (1967), *A New Introduction to Philosophy* (1971), and *The Eclipse of Excellence: A Critique of American Higher Education* (1973). He has contributed to *The Encyclopedia of Philosophy* and numerous philosophical journals.

Charles Frankel is Old Dominion Professor of Philosophy and Public Affairs at Columbia University, where he teaches in the Department of Philosophy and the School of Law. His books include *The Case for Modern Man* (1955), *The Democratic Prospect* (1962), *Education and the Barricades* (1968), and *The Pleasures of Philosophy* (1972). He has been Assistant Secretary of State for Educational and Cultural Affairs of the United States and Chairman of the Committee on Professional Ethics at the American Association of University Professors. At present he is Chairman of the International Council on the Future of the University.

Mortimer Kadish is Professor of Philosophy and Chairman of the Department at Case Western Reserve University. He is the author of *Reason and Controversy in the Arts* (1968), and the co-author (with S. H. Kadish) of *Discretion to Disobey: A Study of Lawful Departures From Legal Rules* (1973). His articles have appeared in numerous philosophical journals, and he has also published a novel, *Point of Honor*, and a number of short stories. He has received fellowships from the Guggenheim Foundation, the American Council of Learned Societies, and the Rockefeller Foundation.

Joseph Margolis is Professor of Philosophy at Temple University. He has taught widely in the United States and Canada. Among his recent publications are: *Values and Conduct* (1971); *Knowledge and Existence* (1973); *Negativities, The Limits of Life* (1975). He will be publishing shortly a considerably revised version of his *The Language of Art and Art Criticism;* and he has recently completed a new book, *Persons and Minds*.

Frederick A. Olafson was previously Professor of Education and Philosophy at Harvard University and is currently Professor of Philosophy and Chairman of the Department at the University of California, San Diego. He is the author of *Principles and Persons: An Ethical Interpretation of Existentialism* (1967) and *Ethics and Twentieth Century Thought* (1973), as well as of a number of articles dealing with philosophical aspects of education.

Contributors

James Rachels is Associate Professor of Philosophy at the University of Miami in Coral Gables. He is the editor of *Moral Problems* (second edition, 1975) and has contributed articles on ethics to various philosophical journals. He is a past chairman of the Society for Philosophy and Public Affairs.

Richard Rorty taught at Yale and at Wellesley, and since 1961 he has been a member of the Department of Philosophy at Princeton University. He has written articles on various topics in history of philosophy, the philosophy of mind, and metaphilosophy. He is the editor of *The Linguistic Turn: Recent Essays in Philosophic Method* (1967).

New Studies in the
Philosophy of John Dewey

1

John Dewey's Social Philosophy

CHARLES FRANKEL

IN 1903, when John Dewey was teaching at the University of Chicago, William James remarked in a letter:

> Chicago University has during the past six months given birth to the fruit of its ten years of gestation under John Dewey. The result is wonderful—a *real school*, and *real Thought*. Important thought, too! Did you ever hear of such a city or such a University? Here [at Harvard] we have thought, but no school. At Yale a school but no thought. Chicago has both.[1]

Probably no American philosopher has ever exercised so much practical influence as John Dewey. Not many philosophers have done so anywhere. He made the universities with which he was associated, Chicago and Columbia, symbols of the hope that the nonsense could be shaken out of society's beliefs, and that intelligence could shame or tame the holders of power. And his influence moved far beyond these universities. Until the fifties, people who had learned their philosophical ABC's from Dewey or his students were dominant in American legal realism, in institutional economics, in social psychology and political science, in reforms of liberal and professional education, and in the teachers' colleges and the schools.

How did Dewey come to exercise this influence? He was not a zealot or an organizer of movements. The answer, I think, is that he offered, as no one else did in his time, what seemed to be a developed and coherent *social* philosophy, a program for identifying what was wrong with American life and for reconstructing American institutions and the habits of thought that lay behind them. But did Dewey's philosophy really do what its many adherents thought it did? And where can we stand today in relation to this philosophy? A Deluge —two, three, or four Deluges—stand between us and the days when Dewey exercised his greatest influence. Philosophy has changed. American politics and intellectual life have changed. Our social hopes and passions have been put to terrible tests. Is Dewey's philosophy still a source of useful instruction, or should it be put aside as the expression of an intellectually soft and politically innocent era?

1

When Dewey was eighty, he engaged in a debate, at a meeting of the American Philosophical Association, with his old friend and Columbia colleague, William Pepperell Montague, in the course of which Montague complimented him for his lifelong effort to practicalize intelligence. Dewey replied quietly but firmly that Montague was taking a narrow, inbred view—a philosopher's trade-union view, he implied—of what he, Dewey, had tried to accomplish. His effort had not been to practicalize intelligence but to intellectualize practice.

Dewey was entirely unabashed in his conviction that philosophers exist not to solve their own special technical problems, but to throw light on the problems of men in society. For him, the technical side of philosophy was important, but only as it contributed to philosophy's larger social purpose. Although he was not an angry polemicist, he was sometimes only barely diplomatic in his expression of amusement or impatience at the pretention of professional philosophers to be exploring a realm of timeless truth above the battle. For him all philosophy was at bottom social philosophy implicitly or explicitly. Radical though he was in his critique of what he called "the classic tradition" in philosophy, he revived a classical Greek view of philosophy. He saw it as a civic enterprise. He identified philosophy as the critique of a civilization and the instrument for guiding historical change intelligently. As he wrote in *Philosophy and Civilization*, philosophy's "connection with social history, with civilization, is intrinsic."[2] And as he said in *The Quest for Certainty*, "Only upon the obverse of the adage that whoso drives fat oxen must himself be fat, can it be urged that logical austerity of personal attitude and procedure demands that the subject-matter dealt with [by philosophy] must be made lean by stripping it of all that is human concern."[3] Dewey, in short, did not merely offer a social philosophy as part of a larger philosophy. He offered a philosophy that was nothing if it was not, in its entirety, a social philosophy.

Accordingly, there is a troublesome paradox with which any examination of Dewey's social philosophy has to begin. Perhaps because Dewey's social philosophy is everywhere in his works, it is not easy to find it in any particular place. In the conventional sense of the term, Dewey had no social philosophy, or next to none. His books contain few extended analyses of concepts like liberty, equality, or justice, or of basic social phenomena like class, property, power, interest groups, political bargaining, the military establishments, or bureaucracy. On the whole, Dewey touched such matters, when he touched them at all, with a quick brush and a passing allusion. Nor did he deal in an explicit and systematic way with the major social thinkers of his era. There is no sustained comment by him anywhere on the status or meaning of Freud's theories for social thought and practice—this despite the fact that Dewey was interested in education and child development, and constantly emphasized the close relationship between the development of the cognitive and affective sides of human behavior. Similarly, although Dewey paid attention to Marxism, he rarely met the Marxist challenge head on by systematically evaluating major Marxist doctrines. Neither did he comment with any specificity on the varieties of program that existed in his day for the reconstruction of industrial society, as did Bertrand Russell, for example, in *Roads to Freedom*. Marx and John Stuart Mill, Morris Cohen and Karl Popper, Henri

Bergson and Jean-Paul Sartre have all been social philosophers in a way that Dewey was not.

Even in regard to the point of view with respect to which almost every intellectual in the twenties and thirties thought that he had to define his position—namely, socialism—it is uncertain where Dewey stood. In *Art as Experience*, published in 1934, he sounds like a socialist:

> The labor and employment problem of which we are so acutely aware cannot be solved by mere changes in wage hours of work and sanitary conditions. No permanent solution is possible save in a radical social alteration, which effects the degree and kind of participation the worker has in the production and social disposition of the wares he produces. . . . The psychological conditions resulting from control of the labor of other men for the sake of private gain, rather than any fixed psychological or economic law, are the forces that suppress and limit esthetic quality in the experience that accompanies processes of production (pp. 343–344).

But in *Freedom and Culture*, published five years later, he expressed doubt that a change in property relations alone is enough to change the relation of the worker to his work, and he paid an unexpected tribute to the greatest spokesman for *laissez-faire:*

> In fact, there is one thesis of Herbert Spencer that could now be revived with a good deal of evidence in its support: namely, the economic situation is so complex, so intricate in the interdependence of delicately

7

balanced factors, that planned policies initiated by public authority are sure to have consequences totally unforeseeable,—often the contrary of what was intended. . . (p. 62).

Friedrich Hayek and Milton Friedman could hardly put the case against socialism and government planning more strongly.

Indeed, although Dewey is commonly regarded, by both supporters and opponents, as the prototype of the "progressive" and "liberal" thinker, one finds in his pages outright conservative ideas. In the last chapter of *Freedom and Culture*, for example, he espoused the cause of small face-to-face communities and paid tribute to the principles of Jeffersonian democracy. Similarly, if one wants a judicious critique of the follies of what is known as "progressive education," one can hardly do better than read the brief book *Experience and Education* which Dewey, the reputed father of progressive education, wrote toward the end of his life. In sum, his views on concrete social, political, and educational issues were equivocal, often changeable, and (despite the efforts of some of his enthusiastic apostles) never summarizable in a neat form. Indeed, it has to be said of Dewey that, for a man who condemned thinkers who tried to remain above the battle, his own opinions, in their vagueness and generality, often seem disappointingly above the battle.

2

Was the late Richard Hofstadter right, then, in the harsh verdict he passed on Dewey? After commenting on how badly Dewey wrote, Hofstadter said: "His style is suggestive of the cannonading of distant armies: one concludes that something portentous is going on at a remote and inaccessible distance but one cannot determine just what it is."[4] Dewey did write badly. And it is often difficult to determine just what it is that is going on when he discusses a specific issue, whether in logic, educational theory, esthetics, or politics. It is a serious failing in his work that he did not provide a social philosophy in the conventional sense. However, he offered, in lieu of such a philosophy, something else that has, I believe, continuing importance. It was a distinctive manner of dealing with issues.

What was this distinctive manner? In part it was the reiteration of certain themes and doctrines. These themes and doctrines are not the whole of Dewey's approach, and not the best part of it, but it has been usual to identify them with the whole or the best of Dewey's social thought. And in fact, though our jaundiced post-Vietnam, post *Brown v. Board of Education*, eyes may not see much in them, they have more to offer us, I believe, than at first we are likely to think.

The recurrent doctrines in Dewey's social thought come down, I believe, to three:

1. Scientific method should be employed to solve social problems.
2. The validity of democracy lies in the analogy between its procedures and those of scientific method, and from its openness to the application of scientific method.

3. The primary practical instrument for transforming and improving society is the school.

3

Now, a generation after Dewey deposited these ideas in the American liberal mind, it is hard to believe that they once engendered the excitement they did. When we think of applying science to social affairs, for example, reasons crowd the mind to dismiss the idea as simplistic, almost quaint. In return for the immense funds and effort poured into the social sciences over the three decades since World War II there have been relatively few solid results, certainly few of practical significance. Economists, for example, are at odds about how to deal with inflation-cum-unemployment. Despite the inquiries into the pedagogy of reading, the teaching of reading in American schools is unsatisfactory. And social scientists, when called upon to assist in the work of public commissions, often lend their authority to moralistic pronouncements—for example, the Kerner Commission's to the effect that America is a "white racist" nation—instead of contributing, as Dewey hoped they would, to the de-ideologizing of public discussion. In the designing of their theoretical inquiries as well, social scientists have repeatedly shown themselves subject to unexamined ideological preconceptions and to shifting winds of doctrine in the community at large. Not less important, many have been careless or tendentious in their use of such basic social ideas as liberty, equality, and justice. Dewey's trust in science gives a bit of the feeling of listening to a Strauss waltz, a melody from the time when the world was young.

In particular, Dewey's discussions of science as a solvent of social problems skated quickly over an issue of great complexity—the institutional means for making scientific method effective in public policy. The evaluation of the results of deliberately instituted social programs is an unsolved problem central to modern government. The general difficulty of detecting the unintended consequences of deliberate social change is magnified many times over in the case of governmental policies because bureaucracies tend to screen out information that will lead to negative appraisals of what they are doing, and because they operate on such a scale and at such a distance from the actual area of social impact that they cannot easily find out what they are actually accomplishing, nor can anyone else. The problems of the "Hawthorne Effect" and of self-fulfilling prophecies, not to mention the general difficulty of causal imputations in complex historical situations, further aggravate the issue.

And still more, what are the standards of evaluation? What are the tests of effectiveness? When are costs too great for the benefits achieved? How shall they be compared to the costs of doing nothing, or to those of hypothetical alternatives never put to the test? And how is a consensus to be reached about the scale of values that must underlie any appraisal of consequences not wholly personal and impressionistic? Is the development of such a scale of values a job for scientific method, or an accident of history, or an achievement of the political arts? The rational evaluation of social programs is presumably essential if any defensible claim can be made to a "scientific" approach to social issues. But the unsolved problem of how to go about this evaluation remains one of the skeletons in the closet of contemporary government and applied social science. Although Dewey was aware that this problem existed, he offered little help in thinking about it.

Nor is this the only problem related to the bureaucratic and political implementation of scientific inquiry with which Dewey dealt skimpily. Does the effort to deploy scientific methods in the governance of society imply a hierarchical organization of society? An emphasis on bureaucratic as against representative government? More restrictions on the activities of competing interest-groups? And if a society is encouraged to value science and to place great store in scientific intelligence, will it not use its educational system to favor people with scientific gifts, at the expense of other human capabilities? To such troubling questions, which have been asked by many observers not wholly unenlightened, Dewey's response was, in the main, simply to affirm a commitment to the ideal of popular government and to say that science in the control of an insulated elite was a parody of science and not the real thing.

That his heart was in the right democratic place there can be no doubt. But as an analysis of the conditions requisite for the organized democratic application of science to social affairs the response was less than satisfactory. August Comte, after all, had left a philosophy for the creation of a technocratically governed society which had shocked the liberals of the generation that had taught Dewey. Dewey could not have been unaware that questions like those just posed were on people's minds. But his response to them hardly went beyond reassuring generalities. To be sure, Dewey's answer to many of the more usual attacks on the social use of scientific method was a powerful one. As he repeated again and again, science was bound to have mischievous consequences so long as it was used merely as a tool for achieving predetermined purposes while the purposes themselves were not also subjected to appraisal. And as he argued in his *Logic*, the difficulty of making progress in the scientific understanding of society was in part the reflection of the fact that society was not organized in such a way as to permit significant, controlled social experimentation. But Dewey never described or evaluated in necessary detail the conditions required for such a form of social organization.

Nor did he examine the implications of his view that an antecedent condition for significant social inquiry was such a thoroughgoing alteration in social conditions. By hypothesis, such an alteration would have to be produced by political means, and with only the most uncertain guidance from science itself. So not science but politics, after all, was decisive. In his projection of the ideal of applying science to society the conclusion is unavoidable, I think, that Dewey's early Hegelianism never left him. He treated "science" as a disembodied force, an Idea in action, and not as the activity of particular people engaged in particular activities in specific social circumstances.

4

Are we left, then, with a mere piety? I think not. It is helpful to recall what was in Dewey's field of attention when he sang the praises of scientific method. He developed his conception of the potentialities of scientific method in the years between 1890 and 1930. He saw a society in which morals were a product of respectable convention and orthodox religious creeds; in which the turbulence of industrial relations and the wretchedness of millions of workers were excused and explained by references to the eternal verities of human nature and the sacred absolutes of private property; in which education was an exercise in rote learning and copybook maxims; in which the cultural life of the majority was local and insulated, and cut off from metropolitan and cosmopolitan influences. In these circumstances his emphasis on scientific method served indispensable purposes.

It was, to begin with, an espousal of the rights of free inquiry. Taboos, explicit or implicit, overlaid most of the subjects to which attention had to be given if social conditions were to be effectively improved. The living conditions of the poor, the pressures and superstitions of small-town life, the accepted premises of economic relations—all these were treated either as unmentionables in polite society or overlaid with platitudes it was heretical to question. When Dewey was a professor in the Midwest, scholars were being discharged from their posts for espousing William Jennings Bryan's idea that the United States should go off the gold standard. Dewey's espousal of scientific method was a plea, quite simply, to let down the bars, to change the rules that defined good manners, good morals, and good citizenship. In pleading for "science" he was pleading that a hypothetical attitude replace dogmatism, that a willingness to be guided by empirical evidence be substituted for belief in moral and political axioms. Central to his belief in the scientific attitude was his implicit identification of that attitude with the evolutionary attitude. Human ideas and social institutions, he thought, should be construed as instruments of adaptation. When circumstances change, beliefs and institutions should change, and inquiry into facts and consequences should control this change, not rigid doctrine.

Dewey's reliance on science had a second motif. He saw, accurately, that science was subverting inherited institutions. In the Marxian sense it was changing the modes of production, and, beyond these, it was changing the conditions and content of human experiences and enjoyments and undercutting traditional sources of authority. Neither religion nor law nor established conventions could withstand the skeptical salt science was pouring on their received doctrinal foundations. Under the circumstances, new foundations for authoritative belief had to be found. In Dewey's view, so long as science was conceived to be purely technical and instrumental, it would be restricted, in its effect on the general culture, only to a limited, demystifying influence. If it could be used, however, to reconstruct the foundations of moral and social beliefs, it could serve to fill the vacuum of authority which it had helped to create.

No doubt Dewey papers over difficult issues like the relation of facts and values in his conception of the potential social and moral role of science. Yet it would be an act of hubris to say that his counsel has no pertinence for us. The problems that Dewey discerned have shifted their location, but they still exist. Ideologies abound; the idea that moral principles permit no hesitation or compromise is still powerful; disparagement of science because it merely gives us "neutral facts" is common. The desire for total philosophies, for final answers, and for mystical escape from the restraints of the human condition are major social phenomena—and they affect intellectual culture as much as they affect popular culture. Scientific method, Dewey believed, taught the virtue of tentativeness and the satisfaction in modulated ideas. If this lesson be a banality, it is a banality that is still widely ignored.

5

As with his call for the spread of scientific habits of mind, Dewey also overdid the analogy, it seems to me, between science and democracy. His error was the obverse of the error that is too commonly made today. Dewey exaggerated the scientific character of democratic politics. Today, by a kind of reverse Deweyan twist, the political character of scientific thought tends to be overstressed.

For Dewey, democracy acquired its legitimacy by its fruits in human experience—most of all, by its fruits in shared experience and in the development of the art of uniting individualistic personalities in cooperative undertakings. This democratic art was distinctive, for while other types of society also enlisted individuals in collective enterprises, only democracy envisaged not enlistment but voluntary participation. Democracy, then, was not a narrow exercise in political forms. It was an endeavor to construct a distinctive type of culture, to provide a distinctive education, or *Bildung*, for the human personality.

In Dewey's view, the justification of the democratic ideal, like the justification of any other ideal, lay in the methods requisite for pursuing it. Scientific results were validated by the methods of inquiry that yielded them; similarly, the democratic ideal was a valid ideal because the democratic method met certain basic standards of rationality. Democracy permitted free debate, the public examination of alternatives, the treatment of laws and institutions as subject to scrutiny and correction. In this it was like science. In principle, it ruled out decision by personal fiat or superior physical power; and though, like science, it gave free rein and encouragement to individuals who dissented from established opinion, its method, again like science, was not to take any individual's word for anything but to subject all opinions to the collective judgment of a community. (Of course, science did not *demonstrate* that democracy was the best political system. There have been friendly interpreters of Dewey who appear to have found this idea in his books. With all allowance for the vagueness of much that he said, I find no such doctrine in his writings. Democracy was "scientific," for Dewey, not at all in the sense in which, for example, *laissez-faire* was "scientific"

17

for Herbert Spencer—a deduction from basic laws allegedly proved by science. It was scientific in its spirit. Its method of making decisions and engaging the citizenry in the enterprises of the community was analogous to the way in which the scientific community functioned.)

But did Dewey intend only to argue that democracy encouraged habits of tolerance and civility, and that these were politically humane and also congenial to the development of free scientific inquiry? Or did he mean something more? If he meant something more, his position cannot, I think, be successfully defended. A scientific community is a community of competence, the competence is specialized, and the method by which this community functions involves an appeal to evidence. What is sought is consensus of opinion checked against what lies beyond opinion. In none of these respects is democracy "scientific" in its method. Although it places certain restrictions on its membership, such as adulthood and citizenship, the democratic community of decision-makers is not a community of specialized competence. And what is sought is a consensus that is a consensus of opinions and interests, whether or not evidence can be produced in its support. The validation of this consensus comes not from its correspondence with putatively independent facts but from its fidelity to stated constitutional procedures. To be sure, democracy may well be a better method than authoritarianism for producing a consensus responsive to facts. To the extent that this is so, democracy is a preferable arrangement. But obviously a democratic consensus can be a consensus in illusion—and when it is broken, it may be only because a new consensus in illusion has taken its place, and not because an awareness of fact has penetrated the communal consciousness. Nor does the justification of the validating constitutional procedures involve showing that they are analogous to scientific models of sound procedure. The justification, if there is one, lies in pointing to their efficiency in producing an operative consensus and to their moral and intellectual consequences in the lives of citizens.

The issue is not a minor one. As Mill, Tocqueville, Weber, Santayana, and, before them, Plato and Aristotle have pointed out, *more* democracy—more participation, more expression of the popular will, more equality—does not inevitably mean either more intellectual liberty or more science. It could mean less. The tension between liberty and democracy is one to which Dewey rarely addressed himself. It was this tension that led Santayana, in his early, more sympathetic treatment of democracy in *Reason in Society*, to say, "If a noble and civilized democracy is to subsist, the common citizen must be something of a saint and something of a hero. We see therefore now justly flattering and profound, and at the same time, how ominous, was Montesquieu's saying that the principle of democracy was virtue."[5] There is the flavor, sometimes, in Dewey's reflections on democracy, particularly his earlier ones, of a kind of textbookish rationalism and humanism.

Furthermore, the assimilation of democracy to science confuses the categories of judgment. The tendency to justify democracy by calling it scientific leads either to a

19

distortion of the facts about democracy or to an unnecessary sense of uneasiness when the facts are accurately described. It lays down an inappropriate standard for judging democracy's achievements or failures. Democracy is a procedure for melding and balancing human interests. The process need not be conducted, and at its best is not conducted, without some regard to truth and facts. It may well be self-destructive if it steadily ignores facts. But a democratic polity is not a university, a scientific discipline, or a debating club. Its controlling purpose is collective action, not the accreditation of propositions as true.

To be sure, here as elsewhere Dewey's repeated warning against drawing sharp dichotomies is useful counsel. Highly abstract distinctions are often made between science and politics which obscure the fact that both are human enterprises and have significant characteristics in common. Politics is frequently described, without qualification, as a contest for power; science, in contrast, is described as a cooperative endeavor to discover truth. In fact, however, politics, when stabilized and humane, is a contest for power within the framework of certain common ideals and norms of conduct. (In many democratic countries, furthermore, and not least in the United States, there has been increasing reliance by the courts, legislative chambers, government agencies, and political parties on what are hoped to be impartial inquiries into the facts.) Conversely, as Thomas Kuhn has most recently driven home, vested interests in established paradigms, not to speak of considerations of prestige and personal advantage, play an important role in the evolution of scientific opinion.[6] Thus, there is an intellectual side to politics and a political side to science. We owe much of our present awareness of these facts to Dewey's seminal insights.

Nevertheless, despite some recent efforts to show the contrary, these insights do not obliterate the difference between science and politics. The means–end relationships are different in the two domains. It is not a contradiction in terms to say, as Dewey himself said, that the scientific ingredient in politics, though it is only a means to a larger end, is a praiseworthy means which ought to be employed more than it is. On the other hand, to say that the political ingredient in science should be expanded is immediately to raise the question whether this does not require the abandonment of distinctive scientific goals.[7] Thus the analogy between democracy and science seems to me more tenuous than Dewey's arguments sometimes suggested.

Yet the analogy, in Dewey's hands, had a special value which the qualifications and cautions I have mentioned do not affect. It permitted Dewey to take the idea (put forward, for example, by John Stuart Mill in *On Liberty*) that a political system is in the end to be judged by the type of human being it nourishes, and greatly to extend its significance. Science, he emphasized, was not simply a set of propositions; it was a way of thinking and behaving, and of concerting the ideas and activities of separate individuals. And so was democracy. Like science, if we follow Dewey's analogy, democracy is to be judged not as a passive creed but as a way of directing human thought and imagination.

Dewey's approach to the concept of democracy, like his approach to the concept of philosophy, represented a return to the Greeks. He interpreted democracy as a system of education, as a setting for the formulation of personality, in effect recapturing the classic notion of *Paideia*. He applied to democracy, and specifically to its American version, what was implicit in Pericles' proud boast that Athens was the school of Hellas. As in so much that Dewey wrote, his quarrel with the classic tradition was a quarrel within the family, as it were. He went farther in rejecting Greek dualisms than Descartes or Locke or Bertrand Russell. But he was closer to the Greeks than these philosophers in his essential vision of man as a culture-forming animal, a teaching animal. The intensity of his criticism of the classic tradition may well have been a function, indeed, of the depth of his attachment to it. He called Plato his favorite philosopher.[8]

Undoubtedly, there is a certain strain in adapting the enveloping conception of Paideia to the facts or the possibilities of contemporary democracy. Paideia was a vision of the character and purposes of a polity and culture belonging to a small, homogeneous, highly stratified class society dependent on slaves, and possessing a polytheistic religious tradition and a pagan, Mediterranean moral outlook. Dewey attempted to shape it to the themes and perspectives of a massive industrial democracy with Puritan traditions and a Hobbesian frontier experience in its recent past. Nevertheless, in making the attempt Dewey was on solid traditional ground. He renewed and expanded an old conception of

American society's historical function as "the first new nation." His view of democracy was continuous with the Puritan notion that in America a City on a Hill was being built for all the world to see; it was continuous with Jefferson's belief that America was a promise not simply to itself but to mankind. He believed that American democracy was a school for its citizens, and should be judged, in the final analysis, as a school. And he believed that American democracy might be a school for the world.

In this he was the child of his age, and his age was much like the age of Pericles.[9] Most of the critics of the American status quo in the Progressive Era were discontented not with American ideals but with America's defacement of these ideals. Dewey took it for granted that America had set the terms for the achievement of a form of human excellence that would represent a distinct advance morally and spiritually in the career of mankind. For better or worse, he was the kind of liberal of whom Santayana observed acidly, "All earnest liberals are higher snobs . . . The savage must not remain a savage, nor the nun a nun, and China must not keep its wall."[10] Dewey's comparison of democracy to science indicates how deeply he wished to believe that democracy was universalizable. He did not have Santayana's irony or responsiveness to the particularities of different people's principles and expectations in life. Nor did he have the sense of paradox and tragedy—the feeling for the psychic and social tensions which democracy causes, the alienation that follows from democratic demystification of systems of authority, the clash between the liberal spirit of tentativeness and the demand for transcendent absolutes—which marked the reflections of his great European liberal contemporary, Max Weber.[11] Though Dewey did not suppose that democracy might be realistically achievable everywhere, he felt little difficulty in supposing that a society would be improved if it moved in a democratic direction, and when he was invited by the Turks or the Russians to observe their schools and give his advice, that advice was not fundamentally different from the advice he gave to American educators. His confidence in democracy had an unmistakable quality of provincialism in it.

But is the present liberal mood of disenchantment less provincial? Admitting all the difficulties in supposing that people everywhere can achieve, or should try to achieve, a competitive party system or an American style in classroom education, are all democratic ideals merely matters of local taste? No people anywhere welcomes a regime that practices terror and mass imprisonment, or treats friendship, family, or religion as suspicious because they do not fit its master plan. A relativism that treats totalitarianism as simply a matter of local idiosyncrasy is a posturing relativism. In place of the abstractions like Universal Human Nature and Universal Natural Rights, it imposes only another abstraction, Universal Variability. It is as far from the feelings, frustrations, and aspirations of living human beings as the transcendental liberalism it rejects.

Dewey, though he rejected the concepts of a fixed human nature and a universally valid Natural Law, did not suppose that moral relativism meant moral vertigo.

His liberalism remained the liberalism of the Enlightenment. He thought, quite simply, that if we take into account the character and inevitable limits of political processes and human capacities, some forms of government have to be regarded as frauds and other forms can be seen to be better for the human body and spirit. He was, if one wishes, a Higher Snob. He thought liberal democracy a good idea, with something of value in it for everyone. He was not, as I think the later Santayana was, a Higher Higher Snob, so concerned to show the illusions in all political ideals that he was casual even about the distinction between tyranny and freedom, or between gross lies and milder deceptions.

However, Dewey's sense of democracy as a culture, though it brought a powerfully expanded perspective to the understanding of democracy, did have a cost. Usually he paid comparatively little attention to the forms of political democracy; his attention was on democracy as a style of education, a moral tendency. He may therefore have helped encourage a fallacy, also encouraged by Marxism, which has caused much harm. It is the fallacy of dismissing the legal and institutional apparatus of democracy as "mere forms," as only means, not ends, and saying that what counts about a country is its purposes and ideals. The key question becomes: Does a regime have its heart in the right place? Is it moving in the right direction? Dewey himself did not often fall victim to this fallacy, though he was slower than Bertrand Russell, for example, in recognizing the full horror of Soviet tyranny. He did not so much disparage democratic political forms as take their power and durability perhaps too much for granted. He spoke out of the experience of an age of great turmoil but of basic democratic strength. He was the philosopher for an era when democracy was, in a neutral, descriptive sense, the hope of the world—the system to which most thoughtful people looked when they asked what the future could and should bring. Dewey's contribution was to acquaint them with the moral and cultural range and depth of what it was they were contemplating.

6

Dewey's perspective on democracy as a form of education was of course part and parcel of his predominant interest in education as a social process and moral instrument. He believed that the primary practical instrument for transforming society was the school, and, when we think of Dewey, we cannot but think, first and foremost, of what he did for schools and teachers. Was his view an illusion? Did he, albeit unwittingly, lead the nation's teachers and schools down the garden path?

Dewey said that what goes on in the classroom cannot be disengaged from what goes on outside. As a descriptive statement of the forces playing on the schoolroom, the proposition is incontestable, but it has implications different from those Dewey and his followers usually drew from it. It means the schoolroom is limited in what it can accomplish—limited in its capacity to change attitudes, and, through them, the outside world, and limited even in its capacity to overcome the handicaps that children bring with them from that world. The involvement of the school in the environing community's problems and mores means not that the school is a major engine of social change but that, in unfavorable circumstances, it can have trouble even teaching basic skills. Dewey did not invent the American tradition of turning to education for the solution of problems society is unable or unwilling to solve in other ways. But he strengthened it and, in the process, made the schools objects of exorbitant demands. These demands, as we can now see, have aggravated the school's problems and increased the public disappointment in the school's performance.

But that is only half the story. I quote from Dewey's *Democracy and Education:*

> School facilities must be secured of such amplitude and efficiency as will in fact and not simply in name discount the effects of economic inequalities, and secure to all the wards of the nation equality of equipment for their future careers. Accomplishment of this end demands not only adequate administrative provision of school facilities, and such supplementation of family resources as will enable youth to take advantage of them, but also such modification of traditional ideals of culture, traditional subjects of study and traditional methods of teaching and discipline as will retain all the youth under educational influences until they are equipped to be masters of their own economic and social careers. The ideal may seem remote of execution, but the democratic ideal of education is a farcical yet tragic delusion except as the ideal more and more dominates our public system of education.[12]

The ideal still seems, in Dewey's curious phrase, "remote of execution." It is surely more difficult to realize than Dewey, who did not suppose it was easy, seems to have imagined. But its strength can be seen when we ask a simple question: In a culture under the pressure of the principle of equality of opportunity, what is the alternative to this ideal? Dewey's program for the schools was not drawn from the skies, or from an abstract scheme for a democratic utopia. It was a statement of the problem with which education in a social democracy is inescapably faced.

Such a democracy envisages a steady turning-over of acquired positions and privileges; it is not a settled society but one caught in a continuing process of unmaking and remaking itself. To ask that the schools be instruments of this democratic process was not to visit exclusively upon them the duty of social reform. It was only to say that they could not function effectively apart from this process. They could not ignore it; they could not, without suffering consequences to their own authority, fail to play their distinctive role. The schools, if they performed their role, might moderate the potentialities for violence and frustration inherent in the democratic process. That process ripped the young away from their hereditary outlooks, and it doomed to defeat those who were never permitted to look beyond these outlooks. This was the situation of the children whom a public school teacher was likely to face in a classroom. What could he or she do but take the classroom as a place for preparing the young to understand and cope with their destiny? The school was thus a companion of democracy—the companion, it might be hoped, that would make democracy somewhat gentler and somewhat more intelligible to its citizens.

Dewey's educational philosophy, despite the years he devoted to expounding it, glossed over fundamental questions such as what to teach and how to strike the balance between schools as centers of civic education and schools as centers for training people in specific competencies. His influence in education was the consequence of the fortuitous interaction of his ideas with the interests of teachers in search of professional self-respect and of administrators in search of a mission that a legislature would be prepared to support with adequate funds. Perhaps inevitably, given this audience, his conception of the schools' role in democracy became inflated. But he reinvigorated the teaching profession and immeasurably raised its intellectual sights. The idea that he is responsible for a lowering of standards in public education is a grotesquely unhistorical judgment. And most of all, in his account of the purposes of the school in American democracy, he accurately described the boundaries, I believe, within which any effective policy for American education will have to fall.

7

There is more, then, than meets the careless eye, even in what now seem to be Dewey's banalities. But it is when we turn to what does not seem to be banal in Dewey—and has been increasingly rejected as wrong—that we come to the heart, I believe, of what I described earlier as Dewey's distinctive manner of dealing with social issues.

Why was it that, for all his refusal to present his philosophical arguments in a step-by-step, premise-to-conclusion, fashion, he struck his admirers, and, for that matter, his opponents, as having a systematic and coherent point of view? Why, for all his sobriety and avoidance of melodramatic statements, did he seem to both admirers and opponents to have something radical to offer—a promise of profound liberation to those who approved, a portent of headlong immorality and decay to those who disapproved? The answer, I suggest, lies in the philosophical insight, almost the philosophical reflex, that he retained from his Hegelian apprenticeship. He distrusted dualisms. And he had Hegel's sensitivity to the social habits and institutions which philosophical dualisms register and reinforce.

A common complaint when one reads Dewey is that he often fails to answer the question he himself starts by posing. He seems to change the subject, to wander. But this was the defect of his curious intellectual virtue. He put things into new relations; he broke through the misleading categories in which they were habitually pigeon-holed. Was there a conflict between business and religion? But was not religion a business, and business a religion? Was there a conflict between political idealism and *Realpolitik*? But was not political idealism often an excuse for ruthless tactics, and was not *Realpolitik* a façade behind which lurked an absolute commitment to a fixed moral purpose? Like other great social critics of his generation—Shaw, Russell—he saw things upside down and inside out. Indeed, rather like Shaw and Russell, Dewey's appeal lay precisely in the fact that he presented his moral idealism in what seemed to the audiences of the time to be a most improbable form—the form of an unapologetic naturalism or materialism. He represented a kind of détente, at once unexpected and liberating, between the sacred and the secular, the ideal and the practical. The faults in society, he seemed to be saying, had at least one general cause—the separation in mental habit and in working institutions between subjects that were open to inquiry and subjects considered too sensitive, too close to the divine or the diabolic, to be investigated empirically.

This dualism between the secular and the sacred, in Dewey's opinion, infected the whole range of modern society's activities and guiding principles. It was the sign, indeed, that modern society was insufficiently modernized. The split between the sacred and the secular showed itself in the separation of "the higher knowledge" from the merely practical; in the genteel tradition's manner of dealing with the fine arts and in the tastelessness with which the useful arts were pursued; in the glorification of fundamental individual rights in the abstract and in the indifference to the material conditions that gave these rights substance; in the exercise of authority by teachers independently of the authority of the methods by which the knowledge they transmitted had been acquired and validated; in the wall between the classroom and the world outside; in the absence from most people's work of the possibility of esthetic or moral achievement; in the distance between the active political elite and the passive citizenry; and, most of all, in the classic dualisms of social philosophy and social practice—the individual versus society, values versus facts, ideals versus the practical, morals versus science. The most apparently diverse phenomena were brought together in Dewey's outlook.

How shall we interpret Dewey's sweeping attack on dualisms? There are two possible interpretations—that it was methodological, and that it was metaphysical. But if one recalls Dewey's Peircean background, his use of Darwinism, and his left wing Hegelianism, the inter-pretation of his position as methodological, despite some of his forays into a kind of metaphysics, seems the more convincing.[13] The attack on dualisms was a coun-sel of therapeutic skepticism, a warning that there was less in received conventions of thought than the respect with which they were treated might suggest. The classic dualisms were simply frozen intellectual distinctions that had once served useful but limited purposes. But the problems with respect to which they had arisen had faded; and now their persistence in uncriticized form presented barriers to the solution of the problems at hand.

For example, it was in periods when resources were scarce and the arts of high civilization were impossible unless the many did hard labor, leaving a few to enjoy leisure, that the distinction between the useful and the fine, the instrumentally good and the intrinsically good, arose. Again, it was in the struggle to break away from the feudal era with its system of fixed statuses assigned at birth, that the idea of an individual with rights and needs of his own apart from his social position emerged. So the "individual" was set off from "society." But when these concepts were given metaphysical status, they elevated historically conditioned distinctions into eternal truths. Work in fact could be both useful and delightful, and the instrumentally good could also be good in itself. Similarly, if one meant by a human "individual" anything more than a numerically individual physical object, one had to define individuality in terms of variation from a *specific* social standard or norm. And from a psychological and sociological point of view as well, individuality, Dewey stressed, was a cultural product. In the same way, ends did not belong to one fixed and timeless category and means to another. Ends were means in the direction of conduct. Means were ends when viewed as ingredients of immediate experience and as deposits left in the result attained. They were therefore to be judged in terms of moral standards as much as ends were. Thus Dewey, in his attack on dualisms, might be said to have democratized moral and social judgment. He brought together categories of things hitherto kept apart. He put on a plane of equality things hitherto regarded as superior and inferior.

This, I take it, was (and is) the major source of the disagreement with Dewey's morals and politics. Did he mean that a shoemaker's art and Picasso's were to be treated by society with equal respect, regardless of the rarity of the latter? Did he mean that there was no hierarchy of ends? Did he really mean that distinctions could not be made between the individual and society, or between culture and human nature in the explanation

33

of behavior? It is often difficult to find a clear answer in Dewey's pages. It might be said, indeed, that he often neglected his own counsel. His methodological point, presumably, was that all distinctions are contextual in significance. They are pertinent to particular problems and find their validity in their success in contributing to the intellectual and practical ordering of these problems. But in books like *Experience and Nature*, in which he tried to develop a metaphysics, or in the concept of "the situation" which he put forward in his *Logic*, he seemed to have half-forgotten the contextualism of his own attack on dualisms and to have put a sweeping experiential monism and egalitarianism in its place.

His basic purpose was to affirm the view that distinctions like those between stability and change or objective and subjective are purposive—that they cannot be understood and evaluated apart from their use in inquiry and action. But this did not show—as he sometimes took the trouble to say explicitly and always, I think, assumed—that there are no good reasons for beginning one's inquiries by accepting, if only provisionally, a received hierarchy of distinctions, ends, and principles. In specific contexts of judgment, it is not the case that everything is equal, or that nothing can be called a means and nothing an end, or that no line can be drawn between what shall be ascribed to the individual by way of rights or responsibilities and what shall be ascribed to society. When Dewey's attack on dualisms is interpreted as a denial that such distinctions have presumptive validity, his social and moral philosophy leads to the puzzles that his opponents have found in it. Dewey is best understood—even if somewhat more modestly understood—if the ontology is taken out of his theories.

8

The power of Dewey's antidualistic methodology in its approach to social problems is illustrated in a book of his which is too much neglected—*The Public and Its Problems*. It is an admirable example of his manner of analysis at its best, and it is the book that comes closer than any other he produced to traditional works in social philosophy. He wrote it largely in response to Walter Lippmann's two books *The Phantom Public* and *Public Opinion*, which had expressed doubts about the validity of the classic thesis that democracy was government by public opinion. Lippmann had denied that there was any such thing as an autonomous public opinion; he had argued, further, that when something like what might be called "public opinion" emerged, it was likely to be ignorant and incompetent, and therefore a wretched guide to what needed to be done. In *The Public and Its Problems*, in response to this thesis, Dewey analyzed a specific concept—"the public"—at some length.

He argued that a public is formed when people who are affected indirectly by conflicts between other groups perceive a common interest in a solution. Sometimes they come together formally in third-party interest-groups; sometimes the State takes on the duty of representing and protecting them. Thus there is no Public in the singular, except as an idealization of third-party interests; but there are publics, specific and concrete, which come together and fade away as circumstances alter. Accordingly, to dismiss the philosophy of democracy as false because public opinion is so often a product of propaganda and manipulation was, from Dewey's point of view, to miss half the point.

First of all, publics, as analyzed by Dewey, were composed of people who did not simply view events from a distance or perceive them through the smokescreen thrown up by the mass media. They were personally, even if only indirectly, affected by the conflicts going on and the bargains that were struck by the groups in contention. They might not know what the right solution should be; but they did know that they were being adversely affected and that the shoe was pinching. They had at least to that extent an opinion that could be labeled autonomous, informed, and informative. The unqualified description of democracy as government by manipulated public opinion was therefore a misleading exaggeration.

Second, and equally to the point, the description of democracy as government by controlled or ignorant public opinion rested on a misunderstanding of the function of the concept of democracy. The concept was in part an ideal, a means for putting normative pressure on what exists. "Democracy" pointed to the *right* of publics to participate in the governance of society. It therefore laid out as a task the building of powerful, informed, and active publics. Specifically, it called for development of the arts of communication, education, and political organization in order to ensure that when a public was affected by social decisions, it would not be inert, passive, or merely latently present, but active and efficient in stating its case.

Whether or not one agrees with all the details of this analysis, it shows the peculiar merits of Dewey's approach to social questions. He took the whining sound out of the conventional moralistic or cynical ways of formulating them. He conceived the task of philosophy to be that of breaking through conventional stereotypes and pointing the imagination in the direction in which it could produce inventive and practical solutions to problems. In *The Public and Its Problems* he showed how to take a large and smothering set of paradoxes in democratic theory—for example, the sovereignty of the Public in theory versus its ignorance in fact, or, again, the unity of the Public Interest in theory versus its multiplicity in fact—and to break them down into definite, circumscribable problems to which programs of action might be relevant. He rendered the issues plural and empirical. Given what philosophers have usually done when they have made their contributions to the discussion of political affairs, this was not a minor accomplishment.[14]

In relation to facts and values, the second major theme of social philosophy to which Dewey addressed himself, his contribution was similarly substantial. Here as elsewhere it is possible to accuse him of lack of clarity. He seems sometimes to deny the validity of the distinction between facts and values in any context whatsoever. Yet despite this lack of clarity, he managed to break out of a classic philosophical straitjacket. "Ought," let us agree, is not reducible to "is." But Dewey's naturalism can be presented as an example of "the naturalistic fallacy" only if one interprets it as a general metaphysical statement. If one takes it methodologically and contextually, I would suggest, it offers the outline of a radically fresh approach to the problem of bringing reason to bear on the problems of ethics and politics.

For as Dewey pointed out, the actual problem that is presented when men have values that are in collision is that the conflict consists not in the opposition of abstract statements but in the contest between mutually frustrating proposals for action in determinate contexts. In these contexts people are jointly affected by the consequences of their divided and competing valuations. In such contexts, inquiry may reveal a mutually beneficial means for attaining disparate ends, or it may point to higher-level values not in conflict which call for a common course of behavior. A proposed principle of action is a hypothesis for dealing with a determinate problem. It seeks to realign ends and means, to remake a hitherto accepted hierarchy of goals, to redirect action fruitfully. If inquiry and action validate the hypothesis so construed, the hypothesis is sound. In a paper devoted to a general reevaluation of Dewey's social philosophy as a whole there cannot be room to examine the details of this approach. It must suffice to recognize that it cannot be reduced to any of the classic positions—"subjectivism," "cognitivism," "emotivism," and so on—in terms of which philosophical debate usually proceeds. Dewey broke new ground. Developments in recent analytic jurisprudence—the work of H. L. A. Hart, for example—are in part discoveries, made from a different point of departure, of Dewey's insights. But the new and fertile ground Dewey broke has not as yet been fully cultivated.

9

In looking back on Dewey, I have found it illuminating to compare what he did for his generation with what Marxism did for a generation of Europeans. Before World War II there could be a comparatively simple answer to the question why Marxism, almost everywhere the principal framework for expressing radical philosophical discontent with the existing order, had had only a peripheral effect on the American scene. The answer was that America already possessed a developed and influential philosophy for the criticism and reconstruction of social theory and practice. That philosophy was John Dewey's. Needless to say, such an answer offers only a partial explanation for Marxism's relatively superficial impact on American thought. Nevertheless, it is a not unimportant part of the explanation. Of only one other major country in the Western intellectual tradition could it be said in the thirties—or can it be said today—that its universities, its press, and its major disciplines of social inquiry are free of substantial Marxian deposits of opinion. That country is Great Britain, which, with its utilitarian and Fabian tradition, has had, like the United States, a home-grown alternative to the Marxian outlook.

Marxism has been the force that it has been in history because, for better or for worse, it met certain urgent psychological and social needs. Dewey's philosophy met some of the same needs in the United States. Like Marxism, it offered the disaffected the hope that they could be the heirs of the principal moral and intellectual traditions of the West and yet, at the same time, disengage themselves from ancient pieties and see the truth new. Like Marxism, those persuaded by it could think themselves the adherents of a philosophy at once morally uncompromised and politically realistic, at once scientific and humanistic. It was egalitarian without depreciating the special role of intellectuals; it took its intellectual direction from evolutionary theory and yet somehow seemed to avoid the pitfalls of sheer moral relativism and the worship of power; and despite its flat rejection of traditional religion, it took, like Marxism, a strongly optimistic view of the inherent harmony between mankind's needs and the structure of the cosmos. Dewey spoke less militantly and with incomparably more humility than Marx. Nevertheless, for those who wanted a message the message was there: follow these insights and you enter a realm of freedom: you can subdue blind historical forces, you can put mankind in charge of its destiny.

I do not introduce this comparison with Marxism in order to suggest that Dewey, like Marx, has suffered from enthusiastic disciples who have converted his philosophy into a form of True Belief. The statement is true, but it is not my point. Still less do I wish to say that the sum and substance of Dewey's contribution to American life and culture was that he offered an American form of the Marxian snake juice, and thus helped keep Marxism away from these shores. Dewey's philosophy is distorted when it is treated as an American reply to Marx, or as an episode in the history of ideological confrontation between liberalism and Marxism. His interests and ideas had matured long before the Russian Revolution, and he wrote with only occasional attention to the impact of that revolution on the evolution of events in other countries. But I believe that the comparison between the functions that Dewey's philosophy served and those that Marxism has served brings out two large facts about Dewey with which it is illuminating to conclude.

First, he walked a very narrow line between philosophy conceived as a technique of self-criticism and social reconstruction and philosophy conceived as an ideology. Given the needs of his time—given the needs of any time—it should not be surprising that his systematic antidogmatism was converted by enthusiasts into a new dogmatism it should not be surprising that Dewey himself, though never an ideologue, did sound occasionally like a humanistic minister affirming the powers of positive thinking. But only occasionally. It is a measure of the magnificence of Dewey's achievement that he so rarely fell off the line he drew for himself. He knew very well what he wished to do: he wished to offer his generation of Americans a vision—an image of moral possibility that could give their lives meaning, a coherent view of the relationship between intelligence and conscience, practicalities and ideals—that would allow them to live with integrity. He thought that philosophy must offer something more than mere methodology or verbal disputation. Yet he did not substitute evangelism for philosophy. He showed by his own example that it was possible to be liberal, self-critical, never wholly attached to any partisan cause, and yet to possess an outlook that could give an intelligent human being steadiness and a sense of dedication.

Second, Dewey offered a vision of philosophy itself. He reassigned to the discipline its classic function as the subject that teaches the community how to govern itself.

And he did this even while reviving the Socratic conception of philosophy as the discipline that teaches men how
to ask fresh questions, not the discipline that gives them
firm answers. Since World War II Anglo-American philosophy has moved in a direction opposed, for the most part,
to that which Dewey hoped philosophy would take. For a
considerable period, indeed, the question was seriously
asked, "Is social philosophy a legitimate intellectual pursuit?" and the dominant answer was that it was not. That
period ended in the political conflagrations of the sixties.
But in the main it was the triumph of new ideologies (or
mildly refurbished old ones) that brought social philosophy back to respectability; it was not a vision of philosophy as an instrument of Socratic social criticism. Nevertheless, the ground has been prepared, I think, for a
renewed appreciation of Dewey's vision of philosophy.

Today one can perhaps see the first flickerings of
philosophic second thoughts—second thoughts about the
conception of philosophy which denies its role in social
criticism, and second thoughts about the conception of
philosophy as a discipline that can pull the answers to
complex social problems out of the a priori hat. And as
philosophers pursue these second thoughts, they may find
themselves retracing paths that Dewey once took. What
are the choices for philosophy today? What are the conditions for philosophical self-respect? For philosophy to be
regarded as an intellectually legitimate discipline must it
be a discipline of linguistic analysis or logical formalisms
alone? For philosophy to be socially responsible must it
be simply the subject that offers an a priori warrant for
people's political or moral commitments? Dewey thought

there was another option besides these. If for no other reason, he has something of importance to say to the present generation of philosophers, and something of even greater importance to say to liberal society in its present crisis.

Notes

1. Letter to Mrs. Henry Whitman, October 29, 1903. In *Letters of William James* (Boston, Atlantic Monthly Press, 1920), Vol. 2, pp. 201–202. Quoted by Darnell Rucker, *The Chicago Pragmatists* (Minneapolis, University of Minnesota Press, 1969), p. 3.

2. *Philosophy and Civilization* (New York, Minton, Balch, 1931), p. 3.

3. *The Quest for Certainty* (New York, Minton, Balch, 1929), p. 68.

4. *Anti-Intellectualism in American Life* (New York, Alfred A. Knopf, 1964), p. 361.

5. *The Life of Reason* (New York, Charles Scribner's Sons, 1936), Vol. 2, p. 136.

6. "The Structure of Scientific Revolutions," in *International Encyclopedia of Unified Science* (Chicago, University of Chicago Press, 1962).

7. In this respect, I am inclined to think, Dewey was more moderate and sensible than many of those who today put forth views in some respects superficially like his. Arguments presented in recent years by Paul Feyerabend and others push in the direction of saying that scientific opinion at any given moment is simply an accredited tribal prejudice, a consensus around a set of conventions. This is not the place to discuss these views. But while Dewey's concept of "the situation" lends itself to such attempts to break down the line between "internal" and "external," "subjective" and "objective," Dewey himself never pushed it to the point of denying "Fact" in Charles Peirce's sense of the term.

8. "Were it possible for me to be a devotee of any system, I still should believe that there is greater richness and greater variety of insight in Hegel than in any other single systematic philosopher—though when I say this I exclude Plato, who still provides my favorite

philosophic reading." "From Absolution to Experimentalism," in G. P. Adams and W. P. Montague, *Contemporary American Philosophy* (New York, Macmillan, 1930), Vol. 2, p. 21.

9. Compare the sentiments of another academic reformer who was Dewey's contemporary. On the Fourth of July, 1914, Woodrow Wilson, as President, said: "My dream is that as the years go on and the world knows more and more of America it will also drink at these fountains of youth and renewal . . . I do not know that there will ever be a declaration of independence and of grievances for mankind, but I believe that if such a document is ever drawn it will be drawn in the spirit of the American Declaration of Independence." Quoted by Elmer Bendiner, *A Time for Angels* (New York, Alfred A. Knopf, 1975), p. 11.

10. "The Irony of Liberalism," in *Soliloquies in England* (New York, Charles Scribner's Sons, 1922), p. 181.

11. See the article by Avery Leiserson, "Charles Merriam, Max Weber, and the Search for Synthesis in Political Science," *American Political Science Review*, 69 (1975), 175–185.

12. *Democracy and Education* (New York, Macmillan, 1916), p. 114.

13. "The influence of Darwin upon philosophy resides in his having conquered the phenomena of life for the principle of transition . . . [In] that intellectual transformation affected by the Darwinian logic . . . interest shifts from the wholesale essence back of special changes to the question of how special changes serve and defeat concrete purposes . . ." Dewey, "The Influence of Darwinism on Modern Philosophy," in *The Influence of Darwin on Philosophy* (New York, Henry Holt, 1910), pp. 8–9, 15.

14. "Philosophers . . . have never conceived a theory of politics which could be turned to use, but only such as might be taken for a chimera or might have been formed in Utopia . . . Accordingly, as in all sciences which have a useful application, so especially in that of politics, theory is supposed to be of variance with practice; and no men are esteemed less fit to direct public affairs than theorists or philosophers." This is not Dewey but Spinoza, in the introduction to his *Political Treatise*.

2

Dewey's Metaphysics

RICHARD RORTY

VERY near the end of his life, Dewey hoped to write a new edition of *Experience and Nature*, "changing the title as well as the subject matter from *Nature and Experience* [sic] to *Nature and Culture*." In a letter to Bentley, he says

> I was dumb not to have seen the need for such a shift when the old text was written. I was still hopeful that the philosophic word "Experience" could be redeemed by being returned to its idiomatic usages—which was a piece of historic folly, the hope I mean.

Around the same time, Dewey formally abjured his attempts to rehabilitate the word "metaphysics."[1] As he came to recognize, it is hard to say in what sense *Experience and Nature*, which is often called his "principal work on metaphysics,"[2] is to be assimilated to the genre which includes the central books of Aristotle's *Metaphysics*, Spinoza's *Ethics*, Royce's *The World and the Individual*, and similar paradigms. Dewey's book consists, very roughly, of accounts of the historical and cultural

45

genesis of the problems traditionally dubbed "metaphysical," interspersed with recommendations of various pieces of jargon which, Dewey thinks, will help us to see the irreality (or, at least, the evitability) of these problems. It is easier to think of the book as an explanation of why nobody needs a metaphysics, rather than as itself a metaphysical system. If one thinks of it as a book which ought to have been called *Nature and Culture*, one will be tempted to assimilate it with what, for lack of a better name, we can call the history of ideas: works such as *Metaphysics A*, Kant's "Amphiboly of the Concepts of Reflection," Hegel's *Phenomenology*, Lovejoy's *Great Chain of Being*, and Foucault's *The Order of Things*. Given such an assimilation, one can see the book not as an "empirical metaphysics" but as a historico-sociological study of the cultural phenomenon called "metaphysics." It can be seen as one more version of the polemical critique of the tradition offered in *Reconstruction in Philosophy* and *The Quest for Certainty*.

For most of his life, however, Dewey would not have relished this assimilation. For better or worse, he *wanted* to write a metaphysical system. Throughout his life, he wavered between a therapeutic stance toward philosophy and another, quite different, stance—one in which philosophy was to become "scientific" and "empirical" and to do something serious, systematic, important, and constructive. Dewey sometimes described philosophy as the criticism of culture, but he was never quite content to think of himself as a kibitzer or a therapist or an intellectual historian. He wanted to have things both ways. When Santayana, reviewing *Experience and Nature*, remarked that "naturalistic metaphysics" was a contradiction in terms,[3] Dewey responded as follows:

> This is the extent and method of my "metaphysics":
> —the large and constant features of human sufferings, enjoyments, trials, failures and successes together with the institutions of art, science, technology, politics, and religion which mark them, communicate genuine features of the world within which man lives. The method differs no whit from that of any investigator who, by making certain observations and experiments, and by utilizing the existing body of ideas available for calculation and interpretation, concludes that he really succeeds in finding out something about some limited aspect of nature. If there is any novelty in *Experience and Nature*, it is not, I should say, this "metaphysics" which is that of the common man, but lies in the use made of the method to understand a group of special problems which have troubled philosophy.[4]

In this passage, Dewey wants to say simultaneously "I am just clearing away the dead wood of the philosophical tradition" and "I am using my own powerful invention—the application of scientific and empirical method in philosophy—to do so." But two generations of commentators have been puzzled to say what method might produce "a statement of the generic traits manifested by existences of all kinds without regard to their differentiation into mental and physical"[5] while differing "no whit" from that employed by the laboratory scientist.

Nor has it been any clearer how displaying such generic traits could either avoid banality or dissolve traditional philosophical problems.

Yet another way of putting this tension in Dewey's thought is suggested by some remarks of Sidney Hook, describing Dewey's view of the place of philosophy in culture:

> Traditional metaphysics has always been a violent and logically impossible attempt to impose some parochial scheme of values upon the cosmos in order to justify or undermine a set of existing social institutions by a pretended deduction from the nature of Reality. . . . But once crack the shell of any metaphysical doctrine, what appears is not verifiable knowledge but a directing bias . . . the preeminent subject matter of philosophy has been the relation between things and *values*.[6]

Given this view, one has a dilemma: either Dewey's metaphysics differs from "traditional metaphysics" in not having a directing bias concerning social values because Dewey has found an "empirical" way of doing metaphysics which abstracts from any such biases and values, or else when Dewey falls into his vein of talking of the "generic traits manifested by existences of all kinds" he is in slightly bad faith. The first horn of this dilemma is not one which any Deweyan would want grasped. The best thing about Dewey, one may well feel, is that he did not, like Plato, pretend to be a "spectator of all time and eternity," but used philosophy (even that presumably highest and purest form of philosophy—metaphysics itself) as an instrument of social change. Even if, somehow, one could explain what "empirical method" in metaphysics came down to, it *ought* not (on Dewey's own principles) to be something with the magisterial neutrality which traditionally belongs to a discipline that offers us "generic traits of existents of all kinds." Even if Dewey *could* explain what is "observational and experimental" about *Experience and Nature*, his own remarks about observation and experiment always being tools in aid of some project involving social values should be brought to bear upon his own work. If, as I have said, the actual content of *Experience and Nature* is a series of analyses of how such pseudo-"problems of philosophy" as subject-object and mind-versus-matter arose and how they can be dissolved, the nature of that project is clear. But it is also clear that the talk of "observations and experiment" is as irrelevant to the accomplishment of the project as it was to the great predecessor of all such works of philosophy-as-criticism-of-culture, Hegel's *Phenomenology*.

This point is well brought out by Hook's contrast between the logical positivists' attitude toward philosophical problems and Dewey's own:

Dewey had shown that most of the traditional problems of philosophy were pseudo-problems, i.e., they could not be solved even in their own terms. In a much more formal way the logical empiricists did the same thing and stopped. But instead of stopping with the demonstration of the logical futility of continuing the controversy over formulations which in principle could never be adequate to any concrete problems, Dewey went on to inquire what the genuine conflicts were which lay at the bottom of fruitless verbal disputes.[7]

This seems to me an accurate account of the relevant differences, and also to help explain various changes of fashion in the last forty years or so of the history of American philosophy. Deweyan naturalism, after a period of dominance, was shoved off the American philosophical scene for a couple of decades, during the heyday of logical empiricism. This can easily be explained if one is willing to grant that writers like Russell, Carnap, Ayer, and Black were doing a better job of showing the "pseudoness" of pseudo-problems than Dewey had been able to do. They could do so because they had the virtues of their vices. What now seems to us (in the light of, for example, Quine's and Sellars' criticisms of its assumptions) the dogmatism and artificiality of the logical empiricist movement was precisely what permitted this movement to criticize the tradition so sharply and so effectively. Following Kant in wishing to put philosophy upon the secure path of a science, and writing as if Hegel had never lived, the logical empiricists carried assumptions common to Descartes, Locke, and Kant to their logical conclusion and thus reduced the traditional problematic of philosophy to absurdity. By exhibiting the implications of the quest for certainty, and the inability to resist Hume's conclusions once one had adopted Descartes' spectatorial account of knowledge and what Austin called "the ontology of the sensible manifold," they made clear what Dewey had been unable to make clear: just why the pictures common to the great philosophers of the modern period had to be abandoned.

But in doing this, the logical empiricists encompassed their own destruction, as Austin pointed out against Ayer, and Wittgenstein against Russell, Moore, and his earlier self. "Oxford philosophy," an even shorter-lived movement than logical empiricism, helped us see how logical empiricism had been the *reductio ad absurdum* of a tradition, not the criticism of that tradition from the standpoint of magisterial "logical" neutrality which it had thought itself to be. The narrowness and artificiality of the dualisms which logical empiricism presupposed enabled them to do what Dewey, precisely because of his broader scope and his ability to see the tradition in perspective, had not. Dewey's inquiry into "the genuine conflicts which lay at the bottom of fruitless verbal disputes" had the vices of its virtues: it distracted attention from the way in which, *in their own terms*, the Cartesian-Humean-Kantian assumptions were self-refuting. The positivists and later the "Oxford philosophers" brought these internal contradictions to much sharper focus than had Dewey and his followers, just because their vision was so much narrower.

Hook's account also helps explain the current revival of interest in Dewey. The working out of the pseudo-ness of pseudo-problems is by now familiar. Philosophers would like something new to do. As usual when their fountains of inspiration dry up, English-speaking philosophers are looking to the Continent for some new ideas, and what they find there is just what Dewey hoped for. In 1930, Dewey wrote:

> Intellectual prophecy is dangerous; but if I read the signs of the times aright, the next synthetic movement in philosophy will emerge when the significance of the social sciences and arts has become the object of reflective attention in the same way that mathematical and physical sciences have been made the objects of thought in the past, and when their full import is grasped.[8]

In such writers as Habermas and Foucault, we find just the sort of attention Dewey wanted paid to the cultural matrix in which "the idea of a social science" arose and to the problems which the dubious self-understanding of the social sciences engenders in debates on social and political questions. In writers like Dérrida (and some American philosophers who admire Dérrida's work, like Cavell and Danto), one finds questions about the relation between philosophy and novels, philosophy and theater, philosophy and film, emerging to replace the traditional Kantian, Husserlian, and Carnapian questions about the relation between philosophy on the one hand, and mathematical physics and introspective psychology on the other. This is not, obviously, the first time in the history of philosophy that such questions have been raised; one need only think of Nietzsche, Dilthey, and Cassirer. So I do not want to prophesy that, having finally overcome the Kantian obsession with modeling philosophy on "the mathematical and physical sciences" and with the data and methods of these sciences as principal loci of philosophical inquiry, we are now about to enter a golden age of philosophy under the aegis of Hegelian historicism. I confess I *hope* that that is the case, but the hope may be idle. For present purposes, I simply note that Dewey is just the philosopher one might want to reread if one were turning from Kant to Hegel, from a "metaphysics of experience" to a study of cultural development.

This contrast brings me back from an excursus on recent philosophical fashions to the tension in Dewey's thought which I want to discuss. To give one more illustration of this tension, consider Dewey's devastating remark about the tradition that "Philosophy has assumed for its function a knowledge of reality. This fact makes it a rival instead of a complement to the sciences."[9] To pursue this line of thought consistently, one must renounce the notion of an "empirical metaphysics" as wholeheartedly as one has already renounced a "transcendental account of the possibility of experience." I see no way to reconcile such passages as this, which I think represent Dewey at his best, with his best answer to Santayana—his talk of "generic traits." Sympathetic expositors of Dewey-as-metaphysician—such as Hofstadter, who describes "the aim of metaphysics, as a general theory of existence" as "the discovery of the basic types of involvements and their relationships"[10]— cannot, I think, explain why we *need* a discipline at that level of generality, nor how the results of such "discoveries" can be anything but trivial. Would anyone— including Dewey himself—really believe that there is a discipline that could somehow do for "the basic types of involvement" something left undone by novelists, sociologists, biologists, poets, and historians? All one might want a philosopher to do is to synthesize the novels, poems, histories, and sociologies of the day into some larger unity. But such syntheses are, in fact, offered us on all sides, in *every* discipline. To be an intellectual, rather than simply to "do research," is precisely to reach for some such synthesis. Nothing save the myth that there is something special called "philosophy" that provides the paradigm of a synthetic discipline, and a figure called "the philosopher" who is the paradigm of the intellectual, suggests that the professional philosopher's work is incomplete unless he has drawn up a list of the "generic traits of all existents" or discovers "the basic types of involvements."[11]

So far I have been saying that it is unlikely that we shall find, in *Experience and Nature*, anything which can be called a "metaphysics of experience" as opposed to a therapeutic treatment of the tradition—on the ground that Dewey's own view of the nature and function of philosophy precludes it. To confirm this, one needs to look at what Dewey actually says about experience in this book, and I shall do so shortly. But first I want to insert an account of one of Dewey's earlier views—the notion of "philosophy as psychology" which he held in the 1880's and which became the center of a controversy with Shadworth Hodgson. Turning back the pages to the beginnings of Dewey's philosophical career will show us, I think, both why he thought it was so important to "redescribe experience" and will also suggest why he was tempted to describe that redescription as "the whole of philosophy." Dewey was a hedgehog rather than a fox; he spent his life trying to articulate and restate a single vision, and in the writings of his third decade he already exhibits the tension I have claimed to find in the later writings.

Hodgson reacts indignantly to Dewey's youthful claim that "Psychology is the completed method of philosophy, because in it science and philosophy, fact and reason, are one." He writes:

> The passage [in Dewey's articles] which comes nearest to a description of the method of psychology is the following:
>
>> But the very essence of psychology as method is that it treats of experience in its absolute totality, not setting up some one aspect of it to account for the whole, as, for example, our physical evolutionists do, nor yet attempting to determine its nature from something outside and beyond itself, as, for example our so-called empirical psychologists have done.
>
> The method is here described by negatives only. It consists in the precepts to avoid the faults exemplified by the physical evolutionists on the one hand and the empirical psychologists on the other. But as to any positive direction how to go to work in investigation, there is a blank. This is quite what we should expect from the identification of psychology with transcendental philosophy.[12]

55

Hodgson's criticism is, I think, entirely justified. It parallels Santayana's criticism of the possibility of a "naturalistic metaphysic," and neatly singles out a recurrent flaw in Dewey's work: his habit of announcing a bold new positive program when all he offers, and all he needs to offer, is criticism of the tradition. "Psychology as method" was only the first of a series of resounding but empty slogans that Dewey employed, but it is important to see why this particular slogan attracted him. He ends one of the articles attacked by Hodgson by saying:

> The conclusion of the whole matter is that a "being like man," since self-conscious, is an individualized universe, and hence that his nature is the proper material of philosophy, and in its wholeness the only material. Psychology is the science of this nature, and no dualism in it, or in ways of regarding it, is tenable.[13]

In this passage, and in the pages leading up to it, we get the following doctrines: (a) most of the troubles philosophy has encountered stem from untenable dualisms; (b) traditional empiricism (as represented by Hume, Bain, and Hodgson) puts forward a "partial account of experience" which separates percepts from concepts;[14] (c) the way to overcome such dualisms as those produced by empiricism's separation of percepts from concepts, and thus of consciousness from self-consciousness, is "psychology," the discipline which tells us that no such separations are possible. In his reply to Hodgson, Dewey never really answers Hodgson's question about what the method of psychology might be, but blandly says

> I speak, not as a Germanizing transcendentalist, but according to my humble lights as a psychologist, when I say that I know nothing of a perceptual order apart from a conceptual, and nothing of an agent or bearer apart from the content which it bears. As a psychologist, I see the possibility of abstractly analyzing each from the other, and if I were as fond of erecting the results of an analysis into real entities as Mr. Hodgson believes me to be, I should suppose that they were actually distinct as concrete experiences. But, sticking fast to what Psychology teaches me, I must hold that they are aspects, analytically arrived at, of the one existing reality—conscious experience.[15]

It was not, of course, "psychology" which taught Dewey this, but rather T. H. Green, who had spent a great deal of energy reiterating Kant's criticism of Hume, viz. that no set of percepts juggled about could produce self-consciousness, and who drew the moral that the British empiricist notion of a sensory impression was a confusion between a physiological causal process and a self-conscious perceptual belief.[16] Dewey, however, is not content to let Green's analysis of experience be a better one than Bain's and Hodgson's Humean account: he needs to insist that what Green tells us is also told us by experience itself:

> We may see how the matter stands by inquiring what would be the effect upon philosophy if self-

consciousness were not an *experienced fact*, i.e., if it were not one actual stage in that realization of the universe by an individual which is defined as constituting the sphere of psychology. The result would be again, precisely, that no such thing as philosophy, under any theory of its nature whatever, is possible. Philosophy, it cannot be too often repeated, consists simply in viewing things *sub specie aeternitatis* or *in ordine ad universum.* . . . To deny, therefore, that self-consciousness is a matter of psychological experience is to deny the possibility of any philosophy.[17]

Though Dewey was soon to recant this definition of philosophy, he was never to escape the notion that what he himself said about experience described what experience itself looked like, whereas what others said of experience was a confusion between the data and the products of their analyses. Others might be transcendentalizing metaphysicians, but he was a "humble psychologist." Other philosophers produced dualisms, he was to insist throughout his life, because they "erected the results of an analysis into real entities." But a nondualistic account of experience, of the sort Dewey himself proposed, was to be a true return to *die Sache selbst.* Though he gave up the term "psychology" for his own "philosophical method," replacing it with still vaguer notions like "scientific method in philosophy" and "experimentalism in metaphysics," he was always to insist that his opponents were those who erected dualisms because they "abandoned the acknowledgement of the primacy and ultimacy of gross experience—

primary as it is given in an uncontrolled form, ultimate as it is given in a more regulated and significant form—a form made possible by the methods and results of reflective experience."[18] What exasperated Hodgson in the 1880's was to exasperate another generation of critics in the ·1930's. These critics welcomed with enthusiasm Dewey's suggestions about the cause and cure of traditional empiricisms and rationalisms, but were unable to see much point in Dewey's own "constructive" attempts to produce a philosophical jargon that was dualism-free, nor in his claim to be more "empirical" in method than his opponents.

To conclude this look at Dewey's earliest formulation of a program and method, I think we can see from the passages I have cited how easy it would have been for him, once he had, as he put it, "drifted away from Hegelianism,"[19] to have tried to do justice both to his earlier belief that the Kant-Hegel-Green critique of empiricism was the key to an understanding of man, and to his growing distrust of philosophy as a view of the universe *sub specie aeternitatis*. His resolution of the conflict amounted to saying: there must be a standpoint from which experience can be seen in terms of some "generic traits" which, once recognized, will make it impossible for us to describe it in these misleading ways which generate the subject-object and mind-matter dualisms that have been the dreary topics of traditional philosophical controversy. This viewpoint would not be *sub specie aeternitatis*, since it would emphasize precisely the temporality and contingency which Augustine and Spinoza used the notion of "eternity" to exclude.

But it would resemble traditional metaphysics in providing a permanent neutral matrix for future inquiry. Such a naturalistic metaphysics would say, "Here is what experience is really like, before dualistic analysis has done its fell work." Such a philosophy would thus enjoy the benefit of that "immense release and liberation"[20] which young Dewey had found in Hegel, while spurning all temptations toward "German transcendentalizing."

Some such notion of doing equal justice to Hegel and to "naturalism" lies behind the project Dewey set himself in *Experience and Nature*, and I hope this backward look at the young Dewey may have helped lend additional plausibility to the criticisms I now want to make of that book. The first and most general criticism just repeats Santayana's claim that "naturalistic metaphysics" is a contradiction in terms. One can put this point best, perhaps, by saying that no man can serve both Locke and Hegel. Nobody can claim to offer an "empirical" account of something called "the inclusive integrity of 'experience,'" nor take this "integrated unity as the starting point for philosophic thought,"[21] if he also agrees with Hegel that the starting point of philosophic thought is bound to be the dialectical situation in which one finds oneself caught in one's own historical period—the problems of the men of one's time. Only someone who thought, with Locke, that we can free ourselves from the problems of the day and pursue a "plain, historical, method" in examining the emergence of complex experiences out of simple ones would have written the following:

That the physiological organism with its structure, whether in man or in the lower animals, is concerned with making adaptations and uses of material in the interest of maintenance of the life-process, cannot be denied. The brain and nervous system are primarily organs of action-undergoing; biologically it can be asserted without contravention that primary experience is of a corresponding type. Hence, unless there is breach of historic and natural continuity, cognitive experience must originate within that of a non-cognitive sort.[22]

Again, only someone who thought that a proper account of the "generic traits" of experience could cross the line between physiology and sociology—between causal processes and the self-conscious beliefs and inferences that they make possible—would have written the chapter in *Experience and Nature* called "Nature, Life and Body-Mind," or have attempted to develop a jargon that would apply equally to plants, nervous sytems, and physicists.[23] But this return to Lockean modes of thought, under the aegis of Darwin, betrayed precisely the insight which Dewey owed to Green: that nothing is to be gained for an understanding of human knowledge by running together the vocabularies in which we describe the causal antecedents of knowledge with those in which we offer justifications of our claims to knowledge. Dewey's naturalistic metaphysics hoped to eliminate epistemological problems by offering an up-to-date version of Locke's "plain, historical method." But what Green and Hegel had seen, and Dewey himself saw perfectly well except when he was sidetracked into doing "metaphysics," was that we can eliminate epistemological problems by eliminating the assumption that justification must repose on something other than social practices and human needs. To say, as Dewey wants to, that to gain knowledge is to solve problems, one does not need to find "continuities" between nervous systems and people, or between "experience" and "nature." One does not need to justify our claim to know that, say, a given action was the best we could take by noting that the brain is an "organ of action-undergoing," any more than by pointing out that the particles which make up the brain are undergoing some actions themselves. Dewey, in short, confuses two ways of revolting against philosophical dualisms. The first way is to point out that the dualism is imposed by a tradition for specific cultural reasons, but has now outlived its usefulness. This is the Hegelian way—the way Dewey adopts in "An Empirical Survey of Empiricisms." The second is to describe the phenomenon in a nondualistic way which emphasizes "continuity between lower and higher processes." This is the Lockean way—the way which led Locke to assimilate all mental acts to raw feels, thus paving the way for Humean skepticism. It was this assimilation which provoked Kant's remark that whereas Leibniz "intellectualized" appearances, "Locke sensualized all concepts of the understanding"[24] and which led German thought to turn away from the "naturalism" which Locke seemed to represent. Its reappearance in *Experience and Nature* led the logical empiricists to accuse Dewey of confusing "psychological" with "conceptual" issues.

Dewey wanted to be as naturalistic as Locke and as historicist as Hegel. This can indeed be done. One can say with Locke that the causal processes that go on in the human organism suffice, without the intrusion of anything non-natural, to explain the acquisition of knowledge (moral, mathematical, empirical, and political). One can also say, with Hegel, that rational criticism of knowledge-claims is always in terms of the problems that human beings face at a particular epoch. These two lines of thought neither intersect nor conflict. Keeping them separate has the virtue of doing just what Dewey wanted to do—preventing the formulation of the traditional, skeptically motivated "problems of epistemology." But it also leaves "systematic philosophy" or "metaphysics" with little to do. Dewey never quite brought himself to adopt the Bouwsma-like stance that philosophy's mission, like that of therapy, was to make itself obsolete. So he thought, in *Experience and Nature*, to show what the discovery of the *true* "generic traits" of experience could do.

To make this line of criticism a bit more specific, consider Dewey's treatment of the mind-body problem. He thought to "solve" this problem by avoiding both the crudity and paradox of materialism and the "unscientific" theorizing offered by traditional dualisms. The solution is to say that

Feelings make sense; as immediate meanings of events or objects, they are sensations, or more properly, sensa. Without language, the qualities of organic action that are feelings are pains, pleasures, odors, noises, tones, only potentially and proleptically. With language, they are discriminated and identified. They are then "objectified"; they are immediate traits of things. This "objectification" is not a miraculous ejection from the organism or soul into external things, nor an illusory attribution of psychical entities to physical things. The qualities never were "in" the organism; they always were qualities of interactions in which both extra-organic things and organisms partake.[25]

Such phrases as "qualities of interactions" soothe those who do not see a mind-body problem and provoke those who do. Tell us more, the latter say, about these inter-actions: are they interactions between people and tables, say? Is my *interaction* with this table brown, rather than, as I had previously thought, the *table* being brown? Is Dewey saying something more than that nobody would know that the table was brown unless he understood what the word "brown" meant? Is *that*, in turn, to make the Kantian point that there are no divisions between objects, or between objects and their qualities, until concepts have been used to give sense to feelings? But can that point be made without committing oneself to transcendental idealism? Have we solved the problem of the relation between the empirical self and the material world only to wind up once again with a trans-cendental ego constituting both?

This sequence of rhetorical questions expresses the exasperation which readers of Dewey often feel at his attempt to be as commonsensically realistic as Aristotle while somehow sounding as idealistic as Kant and Green. There is obviously *some* sense in which Dewey agrees with Kant that only the transcendental idealist can be an empirical realist. I think the sense is this: Dewey believed that only someone who broke with Humean empiricism in the way in which Kant and Green did, who recognized that intuitions without concepts were blind, and that no data were ever "raw," could say that both brown tables and swirls of colorless atoms were equally "given in experience." That is, he thought that what Sellars has called "the clash between the scientific and the manifest images of man" could be resolved only by taking commonsense concepts like "brown" and "ugly" and "painful" and "table" as qualities of one sort of interaction and scientific concepts like "atom" and "mass" as qualities of another. What Kant had called "the constitution of the empirical world by synthesis of intuitions under concepts," Dewey wanted to call "interactions in which both extra-organic things and organisms partake." But he wanted this harmless-sounding naturalistic phrase to have the same generality, and to accomplish the same epistemological feats, which Kant's talk of the "constitution of objects" had performed. He wanted phrases like "transaction with the environment" and "adaptation to conditions" to be simultaneously naturalistic and transcendental—to be common-sensical remarks about human perception and knowledge viewed as the psychologist views it and also to be expressions of "generic traits of existence." So he blew up notions like "transaction" and "situation" until they sounded as mysterious as "prime matter" or "thing-in-itself." He made it sound as if what the table *really* was was neither an ugly brown thing whose hard edges bumped people, nor yet a swirl of particles, but something common to both—sheer potentiality, ready to be transformed in a situation. He wanted, in a way, just what he had wanted in the 1880's—that psychology and metaphysics should be one. But the way in which they were to be made one consisted merely in lifting the vocabulary of the evolutionary biologist out of the laboratory and using it to describe everything that could ever count as "Knowledge." It can, of course, be so used. But no problems are solved by doing so, any more than they were solved by Locke's "sensualization" of concepts.

To return to the mind-body problem, the passage I quoted about secondary qualities as "qualities of interactions in which both extra-organic things and organisms partake" leads one naturally to ask: what qualities do those two sorts of things have when they are not interacting? And here Dewey always turns naturalistic and common-sensical on us. Suddenly dropping talk of the "generic traits of existence," we are told that what is interacting is just the good old table, and the good old human body of common sense, or else two swirls of particles, or any other nongeneric description you like. If Dewey had, like Ryle and Sellars and Wittgenstein and Heidegger, confined himself to remarking that without the spectator model of knowledge we should never have had a mind-body problem in the first place, he would have been on firm ground, and would (I think) have said all that needs to be said. But, once again, he wanted not merely skeptical diagnosis but also constructive metaphysical system-building. The system that was built in *Experience and Nature* sounded idealistic, and its solution to the mind-body problem seemed one more invocation of the transcendental ego, because the level of generality to which Dewey ascends is the same level at which Kant worked, and the model of knowledge is the same—the constitution of the knowable by the cooperation of two unknowables. Sounding like Kant is a fate that will overtake *any* systematic account of human knowledge which purports to supplant both physiological Lockean accounts and sociological Hegelian accounts by something still more generic. The "ontology of the sensible manifold" is the common destiny of all philosophers who try for an account of subject-and-object, mind-and-body, which has this generic quality.

I have now made all the criticisms of Dewey's "naturalistic metaphysics" which I have to make, and I should like to end by offering a brief encomium on what Dewey accomplished, sometimes despite himself. Dewey set out to show the harm which traditional philosophical dualisms were doing to our culture, and he thought that to do this job he needed a metaphysics—a description of the generic traits of existence that would solve (or dissolve) the traditional problems of philosophy, as well as open up new avenues for cultural development. I think that he was successful in this latter, larger, aim; he is one of the few philosophers of our century whose imagination was expansive enough to envisage a culture shaped along lines different from those we have developed in the West during the last three hundred years. Dewey's mistake—and it was a trivial and unimportant mistake, even though I have devoted most of this essay to it—was the notion that criticism of culture had to take the form of a redescription of "nature" or "experience" or both. Had Dewey written the book called *Nature and Culture*, which was to replace *Experience and Nature*, he might have felt able to forget the Aristotelian and Kantian models and simply have been Hegelian all the way, as he was in much of his other (and best) work.

By being "Hegelian" I mean here treating the cultural developments which Kant thought it was the task of philosophy to preserve and protect as simply temporary stopping-places for the World-Spirit. Kant thought that there were three permanent data of philosophy: (1) Newtonian physics and the resulting conception of a unified science centering on mathematical descriptions of micro-structures; (2) the common moral consciousness of a North German Pietist; (3) the sense of delicacy, of playful freedom from the imperatives of scientific inquiry and moral duty, offered by the eighteenth-century aesthetic consciousness. The aim of philosophy was to preserve these cultural accomplishments by drawing the lines between them (preferably writing a separate book about each) and showing how they could be rendered compatible with one another and made "necessary." Philosophy, for Kant, as it had been for Aristotle, was a matter of drawing boundaries to keep scientific inquiry from interfering with morals, the aesthetic from interfering with the scientific, and so on. For Hegel, on the other hand, Newtonian physics, the contrite consciousness, and the delight in landscape gardens were brief episodes in the development of spirit: stepping-stones on the way to a culture that would encompass all of these without dividing them from one another. For Dewey, the quests for truth, for moral virtue, and for aesthetic bliss are seen as distinct and potentially competing activities only if one thinks of truth as "accuracy of representation," of moral virtue as purity of heart, and of beauty as "purposiveness without purpose." He did not question the accuracy of Kant's description of the eighteenth-century's ways of thinking of these things, but, with Hegel, he questioned the necessity of staying in the eighteenth century.

If one abandons the Kantian distinctions, one will not think of philosophy as a matter of solving philosophical problems (for example, of having a theory of the relation between sense-experience and theoretical knowledge which will reconcile rationalists and empiricists, or a theory of the relation between mind and body which will reconcile materialists and panpsychists). One will think of it as a matter of putting aside the distinctions that permitted the formulations of the problems in the first place. Dewey, I suggested earlier, was not as good at dissolving philosophical problems as the followers of either the early or the latter Wittgenstein—but he had a larger aim in view. He wanted to sketch a culture that would not continually give rise to new versions of the old problems, because it would no longer make the distinctions between Truth, Goodness, and Beauty which engender such problems.

In doing this larger job, his chief enemy was the notion of Truth as accuracy of representation, the notion later to be attacked by Heidegger, Sartre, and Foucault. Dewey thought that if he could break down this notion, if scientific inquiry could be seen as adapting and coping rather than copying, the continuity between science, morals, and art would become apparent. We would no longer ask ourselves questions about the "purity" of works of art or of our experience of them. We would be receptive to notions like Dérrida's—that language is not a device for representing reality, but a reality in which we live and move. We would be receptive to the diagnosis of traditional philosophy which Sartre and Heidegger offer us—as the attempt to escape from time into the eternal, from freedom into necessity, from action into contemplation. We would see the social sciences not as awkward and unsuccessful attempts to imitate the physicists' elegance, certainty, and freedom from concern with "value," but as suggestions for ways of making human lives into works of art. We would see modern physics both as Snow sees it—as the greatest human accomplishment of the century—and as Kuhn sees it, as one more episode in a series of crises and intervening claims, a series that will never terminate in "the discovery of the truth," the finally accurate representation of reality.

Finally, we might move out from under the shadow of Kant's notion that something called a "metaphysics of experience" is needed to provide the "philosophical basis" for the criticism of culture, to the realization that philosophers' criticisms of culture are not more "scientific," more "fundamental," or more "deep" than those of labor leaders, literary critics, retired statesmen, or sculptors. Philosophers would no longer seem spectators of all time and eternity, or (like social scientists) unsuccessful imitators of the physical sciences, because the scientists themselves would not be seen as spectators or representers. Philosophers could be seen as people who work with the history of philosophy and the contemporary effects of those ideas called "philosophic" upon the rest of the culture—the remnants of past attempts to describe the "generic traits of existence." This is a modest, limited enterprise—as modest and limited as carving stones into new shapes, or finding more basic elementary particles. But it sometimes produces great achievements, and Dewey's work is one of those achievements. It is great not because it provides an accurate representation of the generic traits of nature or experience or culture or anything else. Its greatness lies in the sheer provocativeness of its suggestions about how to slough off our intellectual past, and about how to treat that past as material for playful experimentation rather than as imposing tasks and responsibilities upon us. Dewey's work helps us put aside that spirit of *seriousness* which artists traditionally lack and philosophers are traditionally supposed to maintain. For the spirit of seriousness can only exist in an intellectual world in which human life is an attempt to attain an end beyond life, an escape from freedom into the atemporal. The conception of such a world is still built into our education and our common speech, not to mention the attitudes of philosophers toward their work. But Dewey did his best to help us get rid of it, and he should not be blamed if he occasionally came down with the disease he was trying to cure.

Notes

1. Cf. John Dewey and Arthur F. Bentley, *A Philosophical Correspondence 1932–1951*, ed. S. Ratner and J. Altman (New Brunswick, Rutgers University Press, 1964), p. 643, for the suggested title change. Cf. "Experience and Existence: A Comment," *Philosophy and Phenomenological Research*, 9 (1949), 712 ff., for a renunciation of "metaphysics."

2. E.g. by Arthur E. Murphy, in "Dewey's Epistemology and Metaphysics" in *The Philosophy of John Dewey*, ed. P. A. Schilpp (Evanston and Chicago, Tudor Publishing Co., 1939), p. 219.

3. "Dewey's Naturalistic Metaphysics," reprinted in Schilpp, p. 245.

4. Dewey, "'Half-Hearted Naturalism,'" *Journal of Philosophy*, 24 (1927), 59.

5. Dewey, *Experience and Nature* (New York, W. W. Norton, 1929), p. 412.

6. Sidney Hook, *John Dewey* (New York, John Day, 1939), pp. 34–35.

7. Ibid., p. 44.

8. "From Absolutism to Experimentalism" (1930), reprinted in *John Dewey on Experience, Nature and Freedom*, ed. Richard J. Bernstein (New York, The Library of Liberal Arts, 1960), p. 18.

9. *The Quest for Certainty* (New York, Minton, Balch, 1929), p. 309. I pursue the analogies between this strand in Dewey's thought and Heidegger's criticism of "metaphysics" in "Overcoming the Tradition: Heidegger and Dewey," *Review of Metaphysics*, 30, December 1976. The comparison, I think, helps one see the interplay between what British and American philosophers have made of Hegel's criticism of Kant and what Continental philosophers have made of it.

10. Albert Hofstadter, "Concerning a Certain Deweyan Conception of Metaphysics," in *John Dewey: Philosopher of Science and Freedom*, ed. Sidney Hook (New York, Dial Press, 1949), p. 269. For criticism of this sort of view, see Hook's discussion of Randall in *The Quest for Being* (New York, St. Martins Press, 1961), pp. 163 ff.

11. Here again there is a useful analogy to be drawn with Heidegger. The notion that one should discover "the basic types of involvements" is just what led Heidegger to draw up a list of *Existentiale* in *Sein und Zeit*. The realization that this was part of the "humanist" tradition of metaphysics which he wished to set aside led him, in his later work, to renounce any such project. I discuss the relation between the professional philosopher and the all-purpose intellectual in "Keeping Philosophy Pure," *The Yale Review*, 65 (1976) and in "Professionalized Philosophy and Transcendentalist Culture," *The Georgia Review*, 30 (1976).

12. Shadworth Hodgson, "Illusory Psychology," an attack on Dewey originally published in *Mind* for 1886, and reprinted in *The Early Works of John Dewey*, Vol. 1 (Carbondale, Southern Illinois University Press, 1969). This passage appears in that volume at p. lvi, and the two passages cited from Dewey at pp. 157–158 and pp. 161–162 respectively.

13. From "Psychology as Philosophic Method," *Early Works*, 1, pp. 166–167.

14. For the notion of an "empiricism" as the view in which a "partial account of experience, or rather account of partial experience, is put forward as the totality," see *Early Works*, 1, p. 161.

15. *Early Works*, 1, pp. 171–172.

16. Cf. T. H. Green, *Works*, 1 (London, 1885), pp. 13–19. Green's point in this passage is made explicitly by Dewey in one of the essays which Hodgson is criticizing ("The Psychological Standpoint," *Early Works*, 1, pp. 125–126). Note also Dewey's often cited tribute to Green (*Early Works*, 1, p. 153). For Green's and Dewey's central point against Hume clothed in modern dress, see Sellars, "Empiricism and the Philosophy of Mind," sec. VI (reprinted in his *Science Perception and Reality* [London, Routledge and Kegan Paul, 1963]) and J. Bennett, *Locke, Berkeley, Hume* (Oxford, Oxford University Press, 1971), sec. 4).

17. *Early Works*, 1, p. 152.

18. *Experience and Nature*, p. 15.

19. The phrase is from the autobiographical essay "From Absolutism to Experimentalism," reprinted in Bernstein, p. 12. On the same page he remarks that "I should never think of ignoring, much less denying, what an astute critic occasionally refers to as a novel discovery—that acquaintance with Hegel has left a permanent deposit in my thinking."

20. "From Absolutism to Experimentalism," p. 10.

21. *Experience and Nature*, p. 9.

22. Ibid., p. 23.

23. The sort of jargon which Dewey and Bentley were still aiming for in *Knowing and the Known*.

24. *Kritik der reinen Vernunft*, A271 = B327.

25. *Experience and Nature*, pp. 258–259.

3

John Dewey and the Theory
of the Aesthetic Practice

MORTIMER R. KADISH

AS EVERYONE once knew, the prime objective of John Dewey's long labors was to open up, to "restore" the method of intelligence to the varied practices of civilization. In the tradition of C. S. Peirce, he made science the exemplar of the restoration and the institutional embodiment of the method of intelligence. But how was one to understand science so that, rather than simply monopolizing, as science, any and all genuine uses of human intelligence, it became indeed the exemplar for other practices? For Dewey, the key was art. Among all recent philosophers of major stature who have sought to expand rather than contract the claims of scientific inquiry, Dewey is perhaps the only one to place the image of an art at the center of his argument,[1] so that science itself becomes an art and the presence of art the very measure of reason in our dealings with the world and one another.

This, then, is the question: granting that in an important way Dewey has described how what he calls intelligence might be "restored" to many of the primary practices of civilization, and without harm to their characteristic structure and functions—how has he fared with respect to the enterprise of the arts? Conceiving the arts as inherently social enterprise, as he does (and so they will be taken here), to what extent, and how successfully, has Dewey represented the conditions for intelligent activity in that interfused process of production, consumption, and criticism which we speak of as "the arts"? This representation I call a theory of aesthetic practice; its chief burden consists of examining how much of the sense of other "practices," such as politics or law, might fairly be loaded into the idea of "aesthetic practice," against a tradition that holds the very idea of such a practice anomalous.

My proposal is that Dewey's whole thrust demands a theory of aesthetic practice. My endeavor here will be to show how Dewey's aesthetic philosophy does indeed project a theory of aesthetic practice, but one radically incomplete and marred by ambiguities and difficulties which a greater ·fidelity to some of the fundamental ideas of his own philosophical analysis might have avoided. A discussion of this sort ought perhaps to indicate the relevance of Dewey to what may prove a principal item on the agenda of contemporary aesthetics. In any event, it is designed to move toward his own explicit end, which is, as he announces, "to restore continuity between the refined and intensified forms of experience that are works of art and the everyday events, doings and sufferings that are universally recognized to constitute experience" (3).*

The Triple Doctrine

My discussion of Dewey's theory of aesthetic practice turns upon three primary doctrines or, more accurately, sets of doctrines: the doctrine of experience and aesthetic experience, of expression, and of criticism. They are more skewed, more idiosyncratic than they perhaps appear at first glance.

1. *Art and Experience*. At first glance, the general position is straightforward enough: "art," Dewey tells us (297), "is the most direct and complete manifestation there is of experience as experience." Works of art are not, finally, physical objects but what the art product "does with and in experience" (3)—that is, workings. Art is, to repeat, a "refined and intensified" form of experience. From Dewey's fundamental insistence on the continuity of aesthetic experience with other experience, there follow useful consequences. One ceases to need any special "spiritual" faculties for the creation or appreciation of works of art, and the enterprise of art is turned back upon its material base in much the same fashion that Marx attempted for history. For the conduct of the aesthetic practice, the intractable necessity to say in every case that an object of criticism is or is not Art, and the appropriate response to it is or is not Aesthetic, dissolves. There is no line to

*This, and all subsequent page references in the text, are from *Art as Experience* (New York, Milton Balch, 1934).

be drawn, and there is no reason to wish it otherwise. All this is well known, but less frequently perceived is the fact that one account of aesthetic experience which has such liberating implications actually involves two distinguishable analyses.

According to Dewey's first analysis, aesthetic experience occurs when one has "an" experience. One thinks of one's experience not in terms of some further end-in-view but "as experience," complete and whole in itself. Means become neither sacrifices nor simple necessities in the production and appreciation of art; they are rather media "immanent" in that which is accomplished (197), "internal" to the project rather than external or "mere" means. Experience itself takes place as a process of doing and undergoing between the live creature and its environment, each side acting and being acted upon by the other to generate *an* experience that "is a whole and carries with it its own individualizing quality and self-sufficiency" (35), a whole such that "every successive part flows freely, without seams and unfilled blanks, into what ensues." Artistic perception itself ceases to be a special function of eye or ear and becomes instead "simply the outpost of a total organic activity" (218), as Dewey insists that "in no case can there be perception or an object except in a process developing in time" (175). The "enemies of the aesthetic" become not the useful nor the cognitive but the different sorts of "deviations from the unity of an experience" (40). Such, broadly, is the analysis; its elements run through Dewey's reconstruction of ethics, politics, theory of education, logic, and inquiry.

The second analysis of aesthetic experience adds to the notion that aesthetic experience is "an" experience the further requirement that anyone who undergoes an aesthetic experience construe the object of his attention as, precisely, a manifestation "of" experience. Dewey is quite specific about it: "to perceive, a beholder must *create* his own experience. And his creation must include relations comparable to those which the original producer underwent. . . . with the perceiver, as with the artist, there must be an ordering of the elements of the whole that is in form, although not in details, the same as the process of organization the creator of the work consciously experienced" (54). And again, "The aesthetic experience—in its limited sense—is thus seen to be inherently connected with the experience of making" (49), while an object not so "framed for enjoyed receptive perception" "belongs in a museum of natural history, not in a museum of art" (48).

It is of some interest that Dewey himself does not acknowledge the duality of his account. Two primary reasons, I suggest, enable him to pass over it. First, whether a beholder "creates" his own experience of an object independently of the producer's experience or not, either way aesthetic experience remains "inherently connected with the experience of making"; and Dewey's attention has been focused on construing aesthetic experience as a kind of doing or making. Second, and as central to his doctrine, it will not be important to distinguish the elements of the account if, as he is convinced, the aesthetic experience of the beholder *must* duplicate "in form" the aesthetic experience of the artist in a genuine aesthetic experience. Without such duplication, he believes we take the work of art as a natural object and not as a work of art; we mix our museums. Why must we not mix museums? It is not merely that people have found that natural history museum objects never give the same experiences that art museum objects do (they have not, in fact, found anything of the sort). It is that art by its nature constitutes a primary mode of "sharing" or "communion" among people in virtue of their common condition in interaction with their environment. If this is so, we are as much at one with the creator of the work of art as with the others who appreciate that work, and *of course* aesthetic experience duplicates the experience of the producer of the art.

There is something discomforting about a guaranteed isomorphism between beholder's and producer's experience, despite, and partly because of, qualifications like "in form" and the disclaimers of any necessary similarity "in detail." Perhaps instead of a quasi-logical necessity to deprive objects not deliberately "framed for direct enjoyment" of the status of objects of aesthetic experience one might prefer recourse to a rule for qualifying as an object of aesthetic experience within some rule-organized enterprise. Such a way of approaching aesthetic practice would require, however, that Dewey enlarge his conceptual apparatus beyond the restrictions of natural experience to include rules and conventions as essential parts, hence would vitiate his central project of grasping art as experience. But whatever the problems of his complex account of aesthetic experience, I should like to remark upon the boldness of the hypothesis that aesthetic experience is "inherently connected" with the experience of making. We ought not to forget that the traditional way of dealing with aesthetic experience makes it, in explicit contradistinction, inherently connected with the experience of tasting.

2. *Arts and Expression*. The second major doctrine advanced in *Art as Experience* has art inherently expression and identifies aesthetic emotion with the emotion that "adheres to an object formed by an expressive act" (76). As there are two ways in which works of art constitute aesthetic experience, there are two expression theories, each of which possesses significant consequences for the aesthetic practice and requires adjusting to the other.

The first theory emerges from Dewey's attempt to distinguish expression from statement. "The poetic as distinct from the prosaic, aesthetic art as distinct from scientific, *expression as distinct from statement*" (85), he tells us (italics mine), "does something different from leading to an experience. It constitutes one." "Statement sets forth the conditions under which an experience of an object or situation may be had. It is a good, that is, an effective, statement in the degree these conditions are stated in such a way that they can be used as directions by which one may arrive at the experience" (85). Expressions, in effect, are not, like propositions, instruments. Instead of leading beyond themselves, they function by "clarifying and concentrating meanings contained in scattered and weakened ways in the material of other experiences" (84).

The first theory, then, seems to pivot around the familiar point that the object of attention does its job as art only when it actually presents what is to be expressed, and not when it refers to or describes it. Let us call it the presentational theory. In Dewey the theory entails at least the following positions. (a) Although objects express by exhibiting the properties they are expressive of, the process is far more complex than some iconic theories of Dewey's time suppose; for properties are not simply "exhibited," they are produced in a process of effective interaction between beholder and object. (b) Expression has a unique function: "Expression is the clarification of turbid emotions; our appetites know themselves when they are reflected in the mirror of art, and as they mirror themselves they are transfigured. Emotion that is distinctively aesthetic then occurs" (77). (How this works is no clearer in Dewey than in Croce. Do my appetites know themselves in the Brandenburg concertos? Does Marcel Duchamps' famous nude walking downstairs clarify my turbid emotions?) (c) What works of art express, through presenting the properties they do, are "meanings." After all, what could be expressed in any work of art but a "meaning"? Objects cannot be expressed. A bowl of cherries does not express the cherries in the bowl, not even in virtue of the order it imposes on them; and only meanings can be "clarified." What is a "meaning"? ". . . only superstition," Dewey warns us, "will hold that because the meanings of paintings and symphonies cannot be translated into words, or that of poetry into prose, therefore thought is monopolized by the latter. If all meanings could be adequately expressed by words, the arts of painting and music would not exist" (73).

Meaning is a wild card in Dewey. Whatever the analysis for which one is likely to declare, the presentational theory's implication for the aesthetic practice is at least clear, and so is its problem. The implication is a familiar dogma: any assessment or valuation of artistic meaning that does not proceed entirely and directly from a consideration of the work of art itself must be irrelevant. In criticism, avoid judgments of truth, of moral significance, or of the relation of the critical object to its creator, all of which involve an external reference. Only what is presented is expressed, and what is not expressed is not presented. Art is "an immediate realization of intent" (85). But how shall one know what meanings have actually been presented? How shall one distinguish autosuggestion from recognition in the presence of a work of art? These are not simply theoretical questions; they trouble the conscience of every good critic; they arise in a particularly plaguey way before new works of art; and they vitiate the force of the presentational theory. The problem of "reading" expressions has been brushed under the experiential rug in order to preserve the contrast with statement and natural languages, which do indeed need to be interpreted. I come to the second of Dewey's theories of expression; let it be called the relational theory.

That theory focuses upon the ordinary judgment that to grasp anything as an expression is to grasp it as an expression of someone. On the presentational theory one asks how *well* objects express whatever they do—how "clearly" they express grief, how "purely" joy or a delicate ambiguity; on the relational theory, one asks how adequate the expression is to the expressor. It may be irrelevant to a statement *qua* statement to ask who made it; but on the relational theory it becomes necessary to ask of an expression who expresses himself in it. One sees an expression as "bear[ing] the marks of its individual creator" (92), as Dewey himself observes just when he is trying to distinguish expression from statement.

Let us, then, in stating the relational theory, begin by distinguishing what I should like to call "intent-dependent properties"—sincerity, compromise, skill, success, their opposites and cousins—which characterize objects only insofar as those objects are conceived in relation to the conscious or unconscious intent of some real or putative maker of those objects.[2] Unlike intent-independent properties, like gloom or density in a painting, these are the ones through which we assess the object as a performance. Some say works of art have no relevant intent-dependent properties, since either those properties are not proper values of the works of art themselves or, if they are such proper values, they are not intent-dependent. The relational theory holds that some intent-dependent properties are indeed proper objects of artistically relevant appreciation and criticism.

Such remarks as the following show that Dewey does indeed maintain a relational theory: "Knowledge of a wide range of traditions is a condition of exact and severe discrimination. For only by means of such a knowledge can the critic detect the intent of the artist and the adequacy of his execution of intent" (312), or, on the same page, "understanding of the development of an artist is necessary to discrimination of his intent in any single work." At another time, he speaks of "a trait inherent in the work of the artist, the necessity of sincerity; the necessity that he shall not fake and compromise. . . . Tolstoy's identification of sincerity as the essence of originality compensates for much that is eccentric in his tractate on art" (189–90). The language of intent-dependent properties, hence of predicates for assessment—"fake," "compromise," "originality"—can hardly be carried further. And at almost the very end of *Art as Experience*, he repeats for us, "We lay hold of the full import of a work of art only as we go through in our own vital processes the processes the artist went through in producing the work. It is the critic's privilege to share in the promotion of this active process" (325).

Dewey's delicate problem is now to show how he can properly make remarks such as the above and *also* say things like this: "It is absurd to ask what an artist 'really' meant by his product; he himself would find different meanings in it at different days and hours and in different states of his own development. If he could be articulate, he would say, 'I meant just *that*, and *that* means whatever you or anyone can honestly, that is in virtue of your own vital experience, get out of it' " (108–09). The relational theory must be developed into a theory of *relevant* intent-dependent properties to make the relational theory plausible. Has Dewey provided such a theory? In part I think he has, but only in part.

The basis for his way of handling the problem becomes visible when one sees that there are two ways, not one, of construing the famous dictum already quoted, that art is "an immediate realization of intent." Instead of construing it to mean that whatever is intended is realized, as one would construe it on the presentational theory, one construes it to mean that *intent* is realized, immediately, in the work of art. If art objects achieve someone's intent, art objects, it may also be said, are objects in which someone's intent actually appears in the perceptible shape of intent-dependent properties. So, for example, Dewey writes that "evidence of unusual skill and economy in the use of means when those traits are integrated with the actual work" will be admired "not as part of the external equipment of the artist, but as an enhanced expression belonging to the objects" (40). Accordingly, he is not merely saying, as he would be if he recognized merely intent-independent properties as artistically relevant, that whatever the artist intended to express in the work is present in the work or nowhere. He is also saying that the artist succeeds or fails as an artist in stamping visibly on his work his intent. Therefore it makes sense for Dewey to have the artist, bothered about what he intended the work to mean or to be, respond, "It means just that!" The relevant intent is there, not just its traces so that the intent itself has to be inferred. No incompatibility exists between the presentation and relational theories of expression if only those intent-dependent properties that are immediately realizable are artistically relevent.

Can an artist realize—actualize—a living intent instead

86

of simply the object of an intent? Dewey can at least point out that there is nothing strange about his thesis. Intent is frequently visible in an action. If a man thumbs his nose at me I properly see the action as contemptuous; I do not merely run through the formal properties of a hand held to the end of a nose, for I miss its meaning if I do. Of course, I may prefer to miss that meaning—(what a strange nervous tic!)—but if I do not choose to miss it, I am not therefore guilty of lese majesté toward the gesture itself. It is absurd to say that I am no longer considering the gesture, since I am considering the intention of the gesture. Further, if the fellow tells me that by thumbing his nose, *he* meant to indicate his affection, I ask him whether he is kidding himself or me, or both of us. The intent shines through. In the same way, some actions are on the face of it adroit, some awkward; some are patently insincere; some show an intent divided in itself. Gestures are "immediate realizations of intent"; why not works of art and in the same way? Gestures are appraised for their intent-dependent properties—why not the works of the artist as well? Such properties will be of a different sort from the cheerfulness of yellow in a certain field of colors. Let their phenomenology be what it will; in any event they will not be irrelevant to "the work of art itself" merely because they are intent-dependent.[3] And if, as Dewey observes, "The act of producing that is directed by intent to produce something that is enjoyed in the immediate experience of perceiving has qualities that a spontaneous or uncontrolled activity does not have" (48), the reason is now specific: such things have intent-dependent properties, and intent-dependent properties cannot be conceived as qualities of "spontaneous or uncontrolled activity."

There follows from Dewey's way of managing the relational so that it jibes with the presentational theory a consequence of major value for him. Any theory of expression for Dewey must be able to explain how the arts might have import beyond the particular environments producing them; it must construe aesthetic expression as a form of communication that leaps the barriers to community that ordinary languages like Hindi or English erect through their special grammars (236). Intent-independent properties raise no difficulties; they are just *there*, and if we are not blind, or blinded, we shall see. But human community demands so much more than intent-independent properties. It demands, to link directly each one to every one, precisely those that are intent-dependent. And the relational theory provides the intent-dependent properties he needs in the way he needs them, as data, to be found in the direct transaction between the beholder and the object, requiring no special grammars to confine the community-making function of art. For if A is any artist and B a qualified appreciator, if A fakes, intends, botches X, X will seem to B faked, intended, botched.

Is Dewey's generalization true, assuming a non-trivial and pertinent definition of "qualified"? We all don't understand Chinese; but we might understand Chinese art. Might we not also understand Chinese? A non-trivial and pertinent theory of the qualifications of a proper appreciator may be difficult to secure if we are serious about distinguishing Chinese from Chinese painting. Of course, Dewey may merely be saying that once external and accidental differences among us have been smoothed out we are not so unlike in our experience or so much unlike in the things we do, that we cannot read one another's intent directly. How like are we, then? How directly do we read one another's expressions? The generalization certainly does not hold for gestures, which are notoriously culture-bound. One must both know a great deal, and be someone very specific, to perceive just how, and with what nuance, one is being kidded. It is not clear why the case must be different for human expressions once they are the expressions of art, and especially odd for Dewey to claim it. Moreover, the case for more or less convention-free, intent-independent properties, encountered directly in human experience itself, seems credible in comparison with that for intent-dependent properties. Is it indeed true that even the most proficient connoisseur might be able to pick out intent-dependent properties the way the wine tasters in Hume's example discerned the leather and the key in the bottom of the barrel, with no further information than the taste? I would like to suggest that Dewey holds the universality of the artistically relevant properties not from any disrespect for knowledge and experience in art, but because he regards knowledge and experience strictly as preparations for the perception of such properties as are immediately presented. Knowledge and experience put us in a position to see what is already there. They are tickets of admission; then, once admitted, we see not as through a glass darkly, but directly.

89

Intent-dependent properties, like intent-independent ones, are universal in that anyone can be admitted to the great museum—if he has the price; they are universally perceptible *once one is admitted inside*. That is the Catch 22 of aesthetics.

One difficulty with this way of regarding expressive objects and their properties is that it obscures how in fact we tend to verify the ascription of at least intent-dependent properties. We do so by fixing the critical object in empirically determined places within a complex aesthetic practice. "Under those circumstances," we say, "such and such could not have been intended," or, "How right you were to have seen it as inauthentic!" It is the beauty of a criticism responsible by Dewey's normal standards that even the most qualified appreciator who perceived an object as awkward, bungled, or botched might be mistaken.

3. *Art and Criticism.* It is time to turn directly to Dewey's theory of critical practice and to consider it in relation to his notion of art as experience and of expression as the characteristic activity of art. The theory shapes itself predictably.

The function of criticism [Dewey informs us] is the reeducation of perception of works of art; it is an auxiliary in the process, a difficult process, of learning to see and hear. The conception that its business is to appraise, to judge in the legal and moral sense, arrests the perception of those who are influenced by the criticism that assumes this task. . . . The individual who has an enlarged and quickened experience

90

is one who should make for himself his own appraisal. The way to help him is through the expansion of his own experience by the work of art to which criticism is subsidiary. The moral function of art itself is to remove prejudice, do away with the scales that keep the eye from seeing, tear away the veils due to wont and custom, perfect the power to perceive. The critic's office is to further this work, performed by the object of art. Obtrusion of his own approvals and condemnation, appraisals and ratings, is a sign of failure to apprehend and perform the function of becoming a factor in the development of sincere personal experience. We lay hold of the full importance of a work of art only as we go through in our own vital processes the processes the artist went through in producing the work. It is the critic's privilege to share in the promotion of this active process (324–25).

If it is the distinction of art to express, and expression, unlike statement, draws attention to and within itself rather than pointing elsewhere, what could criticism be about in attributing worth or relative worth, except imposing external and, finally, irrelevant standards? An "appraising" criticism must turn away from expression *qua* expression. Criticism proper will concern itself "with an individual object, not with making comparisons by means of an external preestablished rule between different things" (308). It will issue a judgment that will be "an act of intelligence performed upon the matter of direct perception in the interest of a more adequate perception" (299). Such a criticism's function will be

91

"discrimination and unification. Judgment has to evoke a clearer consciousness of constituent parts and to discover how consistently these parts are related to form a whole" (310). If, informing people of "the outcome of his objective examination," making sure that he does not "depart from the object he is judging" (308–09), the critic helps others in their transactions with art, good. That was his hope. But he can tell them nothing, and not because in a division of labor the critic takes the modest part. As Dewey makes clear, the reason is that the alternative implies some variety of "judicial criticism," some constitution of the arts external to the aesthetic experience, hence owning no intrinsic authority.

I shall call this view of criticism the "minimalist view." The style, the emphases, the eschewal of preferences are those that in literature used to identify the New Criticism. It is presented now through a theory that, making the activity of expression central in all the relations of the aesthetic practice, endeavors to show how a minimalist criticism is, in the nature of the case, not one form of criticism but the only possible one. Such a status attributed to minimalist criticism will repay some attention. Given that even the most discreet critic, who would never tell anyone what to prefer in so personal a matter as taste in art, would rarely hesitate—however discreetly—to indicate to artists the opportunities they lost, their blunders, confusions, insincerities, all of which have as their indubitable consequences that some things are better than others, it seems apparent that Dewey's support of a minimalist criticism cannot rest upon the observation of aesthetic practice. It must, and does, depend upon a series of prior, logical commitments, most particularly, of course, those bearing upon judgments of aesthetic value. "After all," Dewey writes,

> one is concerned with the values of a poem, a stage-play, a painting. One is aware of them as qualities-in-qualitative-relations. One does not at the time categorize them *as* values. One may pronounce a play "fine" or "rotten." If one term such direct characterization valuing, then criticism is *not* valuing. It is a different sort of thing from the direct ejaculation. Criticism is a search for the properties that may justify the direct reaction. And yet, if the search is sincere and informed, it is not, when it is undertaken, concerned with values but with the objective properties of the object under consideration. . . . The critic may or may not at the end pronounce definitely upon the total "value" of the object. . . . If he does, his pronouncement will be more intelligent than it would otherwise have been because his perceptive appreciation is now more instructed. But when he does sum up his judgment of the object, he will, if he is wary, do so in a way that is a summary of the outcome of his objective examination. He will realize that his assertion of "good" or "bad" in this and that degree is something the goodness or badness of which is itself to be tested by other persons in their direct perceptual commerce with the object (308–09).

Whatever else these remarks involve, two related positions are identifiable which confer upon the minimalist position its inevitability. The first is a species of radical emotivism; the second is a related view of aesthetic judgment as response rather than prescription. They are the consequences of Dewey's theory of expression.

One does not ordinarily associate emotivism with John Dewey's treatment of values. Still, if indeed, as he says, "Criticism is a search for the properties that may justify the direct reaction," and those properties are "objective" affairs, such as, presumably, color, lights, volumes, tempi, then it is hard to see how such utterances as "fine" or "rotten" (which I take to be examples of "direct reaction," although he might also have included comparative judgments like "that's better!" or "that's worse!") would be grounded on objective properties except as natural consequences of the encounter with those properties. Judgments, most particularly those which purport to find the values of things, are simple products, and the more intelligent critical pronouncement diminishes into the one that the perception of the aforesaid objective properties engenders. If criticism can be "instructed" by experience, as Dewey insists, no one can say when—no one has need to say—that the instruction has been rightly taken. Learning, as Dewey puts it, becomes "the fuel of warmth of interest" (310), not the corrective. Knowledge and experience, including the knowledge and experience of the variety of relevant considerations Dewey has judiciously worked up in his theory of art and experience—of properties of media, of intent-dependent properties, of the possibilities of formed substances—mold judgments; and judgment so molded is judgment well-molded. The relevant properties that work as good reasons for a critic's judgment lifted from the practice of criticism and introjected into the experience of critics—what more does one need in the long haul to ensure truly "instructed" or "intelligent" decisions?

At any rate, that in judgment of the arts reasons are causes in which we may place our trust explains at least partly why Dewey objects to telling people what they ought to believe and comes down for a minimalist criticism. It is not merely that a tolerant and prudent spirit will prefer such a criticism. There can be no *authority* to the critic's tellings—not only no institutional authority, which is no loss, but no evidential authority. In the consummations of expression, art rises above all authority. So Dewey's emotivist account of the relations between reasons and judgments becomes not merely a metacritical account of what argument is like where induction and deduction are not pertinent, but a description of the characteristic condition of a very special domain, the domain of aesthetics, in which the means-ends continuum and an empirical method do not rule as they do in ethics or politics.

And now one encounters a noteworthy ambivalence in Dewey's views of how the value judgments of critics are to be taken. For despite the proposal to think of value judgments as "summaries," despite the fact that he would like to restrict so far as he can their occurrence in critical discourse—and does not know how far he can —he still would have those judgments "tested" by other people "in their direct perceptual commerce with the object." Let me come down heavily on that word "tested"; it has been used by Dewey on other occasions with a very different meaning. To test a response to a work of art cannot mean for him *merely* to determine whether that response is repeated in someone else's experience. Testing requires logical dependencies. Yet there is no reason in Dewey's presentation of art as experience why one may not stand pat on a response though no one else repeats it. All that is required is sincerity. But experiment, consequence, "the method of science" test one's stand-pattism and one's intelligence, not one's sincerity. They might offer reason to change. That is the kind of "test" Dewey needs, the kind he actually invokes by his talk of "testing" and the kind he has prohibited himself: the "testing" that calls upon the rolling enterprise of preferences, experiences, discoveries, predictions, doings, observings that Dewey has so often invoked before.

The space is lacking for much direct comment on the second position supporting the minimalist view of criticism, the position that a judgment of aesthetic value must be taken not as a "telling" or prescription but as a responding. My concern now is with the logical content of the judgment, neither with its origin nor justification, as before. What does such a judgment claim? The point is that Dewey's expressionism seems to lead him to the view that such judgments advance no claim (although an emotivist view of the relation between reasons and judgments might well be compatible with a view that aesthetic judgments do indeed make claims). Insofar as value judgments do work, they express the personal responses of the critic, if those "summarize" his experience with the object. But expressive judgments like "Great!" or "Rotten!" have as such a very dubious role in critical practice; therefore, if they have any seriousness about them at all, it is in the reasons—the discriminations and unifications—that might be advanced to back them up: in effect, their "summarizing" role. Concerned as Dewey is with criticism "rendering experience of particular works of art more pertinent to the object experienced, more aware of its own content and intent" (309), it comports that judgments of aesthetic value have no content except as signals of experiences to which we might care to attend. He concludes that minimalist criticism is necessary.

Two considerations must suffice here to suggest the contrary. "That's rotten!" implies to anyone who hears it not merely displeasure with the thing but that it is to be avoided. The warning provokes someone to say, "It *isn't!*" He guesses well enough that the response expresses experience. Looking beyond the range of predicates of such undistinguished generality as "rotten" to the gallery of more specifically art-relevant ones, like grace and elegance and—that old classic—beauty, it is even more obviously true that to attribute "value" predicates in criticism makes claims of some sort. Upon this point philosophers as opposed as Hume and Kant have agreed, and made it central to their aesthetics.

The second consideration opposing Dewey's notion of aesthetic value judgments as response, as "aesthetic" in just that narrow meaning of the term that makes it incompatible with judgment as a claiming, is the relation of judgments asserting values to those that instead discriminate and unify. Perhaps it is true, as Dewey says, that we are not particularly interested in the value judgments of critics; but this means merely that we are not particularly interested in the fact that they are the critic's. The critic's perceptions of the structures of his objects do not any the less presuppose a variety of judgments of value, and of comparative value at that: values that determine what is to be looked for, what is to be preferred, what is, finally, to be tested. All this is nothing new. It follows that the no-claims analysis of aesthetic value judgment simply does not square with the structure of reasoning in the practice of criticism.

Some Advantages of Dewey's Theory of Aesthetic Practice

But I have gone too far. If Dewey's theory of aesthetic practice amounts to no more than the doctrines of experience, expression, and criticism as so far discussed, one might infer that the significance Dewey has today must be largely, though not entirely, historical. His contribution to a theory of aesthetic practice has been more positive than that.

1. First, it must be remembered that Dewey's unremitting endeavor to conceive the arts in the same basic terms in which he conceived human life and experience generally led him to conceive criticism in a way more congruent with the practice of critics than his minimalist position, taken in itself, would suggest. If the consummations of art do not exist, and are not intelligible,

detached from the movements and processes of ordinary human experience, "merely" genetic considerations cease to be "merely" genetic. Everything will depend upon how they are employed in appreciation and in criticism. Refocused on the object of criticism or enjoyment in the shape of intent-dependent properties, they provide for satisfaction that would otherwise be overlooked. In the form of considerations of skill, sincerity, authenticity, and the like, the relevance of which to aesthetic judgment has been heavily attached, they cease to be debarred on principle from the business of criticism. People are seen interacting with one another in persistent and memory-laden relations. That is not everything required for an account of the actual aesthetic practice, but it is something. How much it is can be partly assessed if one contrasts Dewey's with Croce's or Collingwood's relational theory of expression. There the product of aesthetic practice is seen detached (except for the feelings it expresses) from its origins, independent of its milieu, without truck with its peers, the absolute intuition. Systematically, the work of art has been alienated from the processes, the "doings," which embroil artist and critic in their professional capacities. The main thrust of Dewey's project is against any such way of conceiving art.

2. It is too easy to overlook, in the contemporary unease with Dewey's way of doing philosophy, elements in his approach to aesthetic practice that might prove instructive. But Dewey manages to steer clear of both the tactics of a purely linguistic analysis of aesthetic problems and of psychologism, while preparing the way for an alternative.

Consider discussions of the "definition" of "art." From the point of view that considers art as a productive process, it cuts no ice that the things made can or cannot be described through a set of necessary and sufficient conditions. That is a serious problem only from the point of view of the consumer facing the baffling variety of the product. He wants to know if he's getting the real McCoy. Reject, as Dewey would have you do, a concept of art formulated independently of the productive process, and the logical problem of the status of "art," whether it is "closed" or "open," loses much of its point.[4] It becomes pointless in much the way it would be pointless to ask, after a survey of the variety of objects in a department store, whether necessary and sufficient conditions might or might not be established to characterize department store objects. Why would one try to find out? Anyone who knows anything about department stores knows those objects are there because department stores are in business and somebody thinks, or pretends to think, they will sell. Aesthetics needs to worry about the concept of a work of art the way business needs to worry about the concept of a departmentalium. For Dewey, the activity is the message. If there are serious problems in describing that activity, in art as in business they are empirical. They consist in establishing a verifiable and practical theory of an actual social phenomenon, the enterprise of art that I have called the aesthetic practice.

There is another advantage to Dewey's approach to the study of aesthetic practice. Despite the descriptive, semipsychological language of felt qualities, perception, interaction, integration, experience, and the like, there is a significant sense in which Dewey has quite deliberately refused to psychologize the theory of aesthetic practice. He calls it "theoretically conceivable that discussion of psychological factors is not a necessary ingredient of a philosophy of art" (245), although he concedes the discussion to be practically indispensable because "historic theories are full of psychological terms, and these terms are not used in a neutral sense, but are charged with interpretations read into them because of psychological theories that have been current." "Discussion of the psychological aspect of aesthetics is unavoidable" only because of the "debris of psychological controversies" (245). I take it that Dewey would want to say that he himself uses the psychological language in which he constructs his theory in that neutral sense, and that he means by this two things: first, that his language is designative, pointing to features that *any* particular psychological theory would have to come to terms with, and secondly, that he will refuse to take the problems of aesthetics in the narrowly psychologizing sense that makes of them problems "in the mind," to be resolved by conjuring up elements that are also in the mind. So Langer is, I think, wrong in grouping Dewey with people like I. A. Richards. To naturalize the activity of art is not necessarily to psychologize. The aesthetic practice attains a public status, a necessary condition for seeing it as a practice.

3. Let us return directly to that most central theme in Dewey, his insistence on a continuity of production and consumption that pervades all the directions and moods

of his ethics, politics, education, and epistemology, and which I take to be perhaps his most fundamental contribution to any theory of aesthetic practice. To be sure, his emphasis on the continuity of production and consumption, of "the artistic" and "the aesthetic" taken narrowly, seems often to be pressed less for its implications for any aesthetic practice than to expose what underlies the epistemological and metaphysical dualism that is Dewey's *bête noire*. Even so, the consumption-production thesis serves his critique of practice in specific ways.

Marx, it will be remembered, had spoken of "estrangement" or "alienation" to describe what happened when production and consumption were institutionally separated into distinct and independent functions; but that same phenomenon and its consequences concerned Dewey equally and fundamentally. Artistic activity for Dewey, as perhaps for Marx also, was the alternative to the producer's estrangement from the objects he made, from the processes by which he made them, and, finally, from himself. A complete aesthetic activity would require, for Dewey, that, rather than functioning as mere consumers, we, the artist's audience, "go through in our own vital processes the processes the artist went through in producing the work." But suppose the same separation of consumption and production that created the dichotomy of work and play in ordinary life were transferred to the aesthetic practice? Then, Dewey conceived, and rightly, as I think, that the artist so "estranged" would pursue his originality for its own sake; his schema of interpretation would become private; his decisions would turn into impulse. The alternative would be commerce. In a complementary fashion, the business of the audience would be to know what it liked and to buy it—while the critic either pre-tested the product or performed prodigies of public relations for consumers who did not know what they liked, by making them like it. He would tell them what they "ought" to like. The reversal of such situations would be Dewey's theory of aesthetic practice. But, of course, there are troubles.

How would one know concretely that the "gap" between consumption and production had been annulled in the aesthetic practice? What would make the annulment possible? It is, after all, not enough to be assured that it occurs in successful art. What would success look like? How would it be measured? Dewey makes no systematic use of the resources available to him from which at least to compose a model for answering such questions. Still, the practice of the sciences he calls upon so often in other connections might provide him with the model he needs. In the sciences no one is said to object to or support a scientific theory unless in the process he does science. No one is said to do science unless the doing and the deed are communicable and verifiable in the relevant scientific community. To think it otherwise is to think the end of science. In a Deweyan spirit one might ask why it should be otherwise with the arts. Acknowledging that art is not science, one might seek in the arts conditions appropriately analogous to those of the scientific enterprise and of sufficient strength to provide a concrete basis for doing away with the dichotomy of production and consumption. And while to seek is not necessarily to find, it does not follow that even if, as Dewey thinks, science is concerned with prediction and control and the arts with expression and consummation, the artistic enterprise will necessarily fail to generate enough organization as an "ongoing process" to support an institutional claim to the continuity of production and consumption in the arts.

At this point someone will answer that while we could never get away with a "chasm" between doing and judging in science, we can get away with it in art; and the proof is that, as Dewey's polemic implicitly testifies, we do. Yet suppose that we *can* get away with it in the arts, the question remains whether we ought to wish to. To the extent that we do, are the consequences for the arts the more tolerable? More deeply, have we in fact got away with it? It is easy to say so if we are ready, as some are, to call almost anything art. But then there is also bad science. Has bad science got away with it?

Assuming the kind of answers to these questions that their formulation here suggests, the basic question emerges of what the logic of decision in the doing of art, appreciation, and criticism would look like, and of how in order to gain a proper image one would need to reconceive the aesthetic practice in comparison with other practices.[5] As part of that question one might ask to just what extent art, appreciation, and criticism might fruitfully be conceived to entail a continuous and progressive inquiry, albeit one not concerned in any unambiguous way with prediction and control. The justification of the question is certainly in Dewey. One recalls the famous definition, cited in our first note, that Dewey offers of inquiry, according to which inquiry is conceived as the transformation of an indeterminate situation into a determinate one—a definition that reads almost like a description of the art of sculpture or painting. Can we go no further in formulating a theory of art as inquiry than to describe the generic processes of the individual's interactions with his environment?

In the last analysis, I would suggest, the benefit of Dewey's theory lies in the problems it creates for contemporary aesthetics.[6] On the whole, contemporary aesthetics has not been quick to take them up, although they are as much, and more, a part of his aesthetics as his theory of presentational expression. Part of the reason for Dewey's own neglect of those problems (aside from the triple doctrine) and for the neglect of most contemporary aesthetics as well, is the persisting difficulty of conceiving how the enterprise of art might constitute a practice.

Carrying On With Dewey

Suppose someone announced that jurisprudence ought to restore the continuity between the law and life, and announcements very much like it have, of course, actually been made under the name of legal realism. What would we expect in the way of a program? We would expect what we received: a turning away from the law as an independent practice and a turning toward it in its dependence on social and political demands, upon the ultimate ends it served. Now suppose someone, say John Dewey, announces that the first problem of aesthetic theory is to restore continuity between the experiences of art and those of ordinary experience. Would one not expect among other consequences—many, like the naturalization of art and the emergence of intent-dependent properties, quite desirable—a turning away from the specific logical and social structures that constitute the aesthetic practice as such? We would expect the features of aesthetic practice that tempt us to call it a practice to be minimized for the sake of the ultimate ends the practice realizes, the immediate experiences of art; cases to be approached one by one in direct relation to that end; no judgment to be allowed against the individual experience and need, as the individual senses them. And so it happens, on Dewey's triple doctrine. The apparent anomaly of a practice that is also aesthetic is reinstated for pragmatic philosophy as it had been instated for idealism.

Yet I would like to propose that the reinstatement of the anomaly may constitute a mistake, and a mistake, moreover, antithetical to what I take to be the main thrust of Dewey's aesthetic philosophy in the innovative aspect discussed in the preceding section. The continuity between art and life, production and consumption, may be carried further by at least a partial saving of the ordinary notion of a practice for the theory of aesthetic practice. What does that notion entail? I have been avoiding the problem, relying upon a loose sense of the term to refer to more or less established ways of doing certain more or less related things. But if reevaluation of the idea of an aesthetic practice is even to be considered, I must do better.[7] Without attempting a systematic examination of the logical structure of a practice, I may still consider those elements of a practice that constitute the major grounds for the alleged incompatibility between the aesthetic and the practical, and test to see how strong those grounds are.

1. To begin with, in any practice rules of some sort bind and define action. But if, with Dewey and in accordance with the requirements of the triple doctrine, one construes the expressions of art as intrinsically individuals in just the respects in which they are art, then the rules for the doing, experiencing, or judging of works of art can at best be summary, post hoc affairs that bind and define nothing, risky rules of thumb. Therefore art cannot constitute a practice as, say, law can, which indeed has rules that bind and define individual cases.[8]

Irrespective of doctrine, Dewey's great sensitivity toward the arts has made him hostile to the use of rules in art to make things or to appraise them. He sees the important sense in which judgment by rule in art must be, and is, completely anaesthetic. What he does not see is that there are rules and rules. If it requires a subtle and judicious study to determine that a certain object does or does not work as art, if our rules of thumb, though they may serve to orient, have no authority, the acknowledgment merely warns against closing our eyes to the subject matter before us. Yet that is a warning that, duly translated, functions as effectively in law or in medicine as in art. As in law or medicine, it does not imply that therefore binding and defining rules—however they bind and define—may not exist at some other points, and indeed be essential to a subtle and judicious empirical study. Dewey's specific analysis of relevant considerations in the making and perception of art attests as much. He would not, I take it, argue that a man who went to a movie prepared to judge it as a stage play would simply be jumping the gun on experience; he would, like the rest of us, want to say that such an individual would misunderstand the way things are done in the movies, in contrast to the stage, hence how films were to be appreciated. The man came with the wrong rule; it did not require the verification of his individual experience to see this, however much such rules may ultimately depend upon experience.

Now Dewey would handle our case by explaining the necessity of understanding art with the nature of the medium in mind. To explain such necessities turns out to be one of the prime businesses of *Art as Experience*. Because art "is" expression, art, including the movies, "is" the sort of thing that works through a medium and requires to be judged as such. The man in the example has committed a mistake in principle. Let Dewey be well or ill-advised in his apriorism: does it not follow that even for him there are higher level rules, rules that bind, as the summaries of experience that he wanted our judgments to express do not bind? He has not noticed those higher level rules only because he sees the rules of the aesthetic practice as having no conceivable alternative, given the nature of art as experience.

2. If, on the other hand, to justify anything stronger

for the aesthetic practice than summary rules requires a deduction from the nature of expression, experience, or some other basic category, then it will be pointless to talk of an aesthetic practice or the higher level rules of that practice. Practices are, after all, made; their rules, not merely their rules of thumb, evolve through the developments of their occasions and technologies; they are essentially historical. Therefore, if Dewey's ahistorical analysis of the rules of aesthetic practice is correct, the aesthetic practice is no genuine practice.

But is it the case that the binding rules of a practice can exist only if they are immune to experience in the practice? For Dewey, that would be a hard conclusion; it explains why he makes all rules in art rules of thumb. Yet there is an alternative, and a Deweyan one, after all. Rules may bind through the weight of the presumption needed to overcome them. To bind, the rule need not necessarily carry the day, as in chess. The history of scientific theories indicates that while they are not easily shaken by the shocks of what would seem like counterexamples, neither are they indifferent to the movement of experiment. Increasing insight into human beings and the potentialities of the natural and social world may weigh more or less heavily for or against one set of preferences for the making, appreciation, and criticism of art, and determine the context in which we approach the particular work. Dewey's own recommendation to restore intent-dependent predicates to criticism, although presented as the logical consequence of a theory of aesthetic experience rather than as a recommendation, follows in the end from a vision of community and a conception of human happiness; and, in truth, there is no apparent logical necessity that we look at works of art for their authenticity, their sincerity, any more than that we refuse so to look at them. The development of the practice, at this time and circumstance, suffices. There is no need to dissolve the aesthetic practice into discrete interactions on the one hand or game playing on the other where the rules are set up prior to the playing.

3. In a practice, experiences and actions in that practice are perceived and judged in relation to one another or they are not perceived and judged in the practice. So the study of the materials of the law are not supposed merely to sharpen the legal mind, or make it more legally sensitive, although conceivably they may sometimes do so; the study is supposed to disclose the meaning of individual statutes, cases, principles, and constitutional provisions at least partly through their bearings upon one another. But Dewey, when he considers the aesthetic practice, sees the participant grasping the experiences and actions of that practice in and for themselves rather than in relation to one another, and locates the value of that grasping in the preparation of sensibility. Hence, if Dewey's expressionism is true, aesthetic practice is no genuine practice.

Yet why, except for conventional expressionist reasons, must the experiences and actions of aesthetic practice be grasped in themselves? Dewey's view of the matter is credible so long as one cannot acknowledge rules. If they are acknowledged, however, individual cases do not forfeit their own natures in virtue of being grasped according to them and in the relations they bear to one another. Rather, that way, in art, they become the things they are. Instead of an ultimate metaphysical particularity—which, after all, works of art share with everything else in the world—they gain what many other things in the world lack: a characteristic individuality determined by their relations to the other objects dealt with in the practice. T. S. Eliot has made this point most effectively in the past, and I shall forbear yet another exposition.[9]

4. A practice in the full sense of the word serves purposes and needs other than the doing of the practice. Practices are *for* something. Games, therefore, subsisting independently of such purposes and needs, are not true practices. In this respect, at least, it may be said, art is more like a game than a practice. Hence, separate the "aesthetic" from the "practical," though not, in Dewey, from the "artistic."

But whatever the weight one wants to attribute to the specialness of art, its abstractness from life, that weight Dewey surely would not care to throw into the scales. The rules, if there are any, for the doing of art are for purposes and needs other than the following of the rules. According to Dewey, the culminations of art are culminations of life experiences. They illuminate life. Perhaps that may be exaggerated, and credible for affairs like music only if one assumes it to begin with. Nevertheless, in a broad way, the impact of the practices and experiences of a civilization on its art, and the art on its civilization, are evidence that art is not at best an obsessive game, that the ends art serves are woven into the basic fabric of civilization and must be found there. Here Dewey is emphatic enough.

Yet it must be admitted that the ends of art are not like, for example, the ends of medicine as those ends are frequently conceived: knowable with some definiteness and clarity (although that definiteness and clarity can be overstated even for a practice like medicine). This circumstance may partly explain the strong temptation to claim that art is for the sake of art—but to say just what that means has proven no easy task. To the degree one takes the aesthetic practice seriously, one ends by incorporating an unspecified and unconfessed spectrum of ends under a slogan that manages to avoid confessing its uninformativeness by denying there is any information to give. Similar considerations hold for "health" as the end of medicine. The ends of a living practice are always in process; only games have certain ends.

5. Lastly, let me emphasize that among the characteristics of any genuine practice is the existence of regular ways of reconciling differences of opinion. Differences are peculiarly meaningful in a practice; they demand reconciliation sometimes at the price of the reconstruction of the practice. Are there no ways whatever of reconciling differences of opinion in aesthetic practice? For Dewey it seems hardly clear that there are or can be, at the same time that in his talk of "testing" he is acknowledging the need. But if there are no grounds for the resolution of differences, aesthetic practice can be a practice only in a Pickwickian sense.

The problem of reason and controversy in the arts, as I have called it elsewhere, is too much to undertake here. Yet it is also the case that if aesthetic practice possesses the characteristics attributed to it above—if, in effect, it possesses different levels of rules, serves purposes and needs outside the satisfying of those rules, deals with its objects in their mutual bearings and seeks to justify its principles and to develop its ends—the existence of methods of reason and controversy capable of resolving significant disputes is no longer an a priori impossibility. Our problem becomes to articulate the implicit logic of argument in the arts and to determine cases in which disagreement requires resolution from the point of view of the practice and when it does not; in that way the nature and scope of the practice will be delineated. That such an inquiry into the resolution of disagreement in the arts carries onward a basic thrust of Dewey's aesthetic endeavor in the arts, his own detailed study in *Art as Experience* of what critics consider in their reasonings seems to sustain.

Let us not end, however, without emphasizing the serious modifications in Dewey's own aesthetic doctrine that closing the gap between production and consumption through a concept of aesthetic practice would impose. There are costs that perhaps one would not want to meet. First, judgments of aesthetic value must, some of them, at least, include among their functions a prescriptive one. If they express, they cannot all merely express; for a practice to be structured, artistically relevant judgments must point, control, recommend—in Dewey's word for it, "tell." Next, if the enterprise of the arts constitutes aesthetic practice, reasons, whether or not they invariably persuade those to whom they are addressed, must have a normative force within the aesthetic practice; there is no more call for emotivism there than in other "practical" practices. Thirdly, the scope of Dewey's much emphasized continuum of means and ends must extend outside individual experience and the workings of individual works of art. To regard criticisms, appreciations, works of art as events in a practice means to see their import not only in relations to individual satisfactions but for one another. Eliot's ideal order, in which the existing "monuments" of art subsist in relation to one another, seems to be a necessary condition for aesthetic practice. Lastly, if the enterprise of the arts is to constitute practice, that basic drive of Dewey's project to grasp the phenomena of art directly from the universal conditions of life and experience must be carefully circumscribed. To be sure, the enterprise of the arts either rests on experience and nature or it loses its seriousness; but, also, unless conventions and histories are essential to it, and capable of change, the enterprise of art has ceased to be a practice in order to become nature.

Notes

1. Consider, for example, Dewey's definition of inquiry which, however odd it may strike one at first sight as a definition of inquiry, seems framed as a description of artistic endeavor: "Inquiry is the controlled or directed transformation of an indeterminate situation into one that is so determinate in its constituent distinctions and relations as to convert the elements of the original situation into a unified whole." *Logic: The Theory of Inquiry* (New York, Holt, Rinehart, and Winston, 1938), pp. 104–05.

2. I speak of "intent-dependent" rather than "intention-dependent" because intention has come to mean in much of the literature that which the artist specifically and consciously aims at doing whether or not it has anything much to do with what he has done—the intellectual backbone of a straw man.

3. It is wrong to ask, as some do, whether for Dewey the properties of expression relate the work to something outside it (the artist), so that they are irrelevant; or whether the properties he means are constitutive of the work and not truly intent-dependent. Cf. M. Beardsley, *Aesthetics* (New York, Harcourt Brace, 1958), p. 352, note 18A. The relationship itself is constitutive or it is artistically irrelevant. That the relationship between the object and the intent is at the same time genuinely relational follows from the fact that the same physical properties can in different frames embody different intents and therefore mean different things.

4. Maurice Mandlebaum seems to have criticized the problem of defining "art" in what I have taken to be Dewey's sense. See his "Family Resemblances and a Generalization Concerning the Arts," *The American Philosophical Quarterly*, 2 (1965), pp. 219–28.

5. In *Reason and Controversy in the Arts* (Cleveland, Case Western Reserve Press, 1968) I sought to develop Dewey's criticism of the gap between consumption and production in a dimension which Dewey had not explored: the resolution of artistically relevant controversy. I think now that my treatment was more compatible with Dewey's than I thought then, when the emphasis on expression and a minimalist criticism in Dewey were uppermost in my reading.

6. The benefit of his theory, it deserves to be remarked, is not the same thing as the benefit of his book. Were this a review of *Art as Experience*, an appreciation of the directness and subtlety of the author's grasp of the materials of art and criticism would have been no more than simple justice. In detail, and in the feel of what the artistic enterprise is like, Dewey may have few peers; he must be read for himself, not for his "challenges."

7. I take it that George Dickie, in his *Art and the Aesthetic* (Ithaca, Cornell University Press, 1974) has in his "institutional analysis" carried through a study of aesthetic experience of the kind that the idea of an aesthetic practice would require. My own examination of the structure of rules and arguments in artistically relevant controversy, in the work cited in note 4 above, with its emphasis on the controlled mutability of such rules and arguments in the development of the arts, may also be taken as an attempt to contribute to the idea of an aesthetic practice.

8. In John Rawls' language—see "Two Concepts of Rules," *Philosophical Review*, 64 (1955), pp. 3-32—Dewey seems to think that all rules are, properly, "summary rules," maxims, rules of thumb. I agree that this is a mistake and there are rules of practice as well. But I do not wish to commit myself here to Rawls' interpretation of rules of practice, partly because I would not wish to interpret the relation of the participant in the practice of art to the rules of that practice, as a relation of a player of a game to the rules of that game. It makes a difference that the rules of practices, unlike the rules of most games, are radically incomplete and changing.

9. "No poet, no artist of any art, has his complete meaning alone. His significance, his appreciation is the appreciation of his relation to the dead poets and artists. You cannot value him alone; you must set him, for contrast and comparison, among the dead. I mean this as a principle of aesthetic, not merely historical, criticism. The necessity that he shall conform, that he shall cohere, is not onesided; what happens when a new work of art is created is something that happens simultaneously to all the works of art which preceded it. The existing monuments form an ideal order among themselves, which is modified by the introduction of the new (the really new) work of art among them." T. S. Eliot, *Selected Essays* (New York, Harcourt, Brace, 1950), pp. 4-5.

4

The Relevance of Dewey's Epistemology

JOSEPH MARGOLIS

THERE are, without doubt, too many tempting ways in which to broach the recovery of John Dewey's epistemology. I prefer a mixture of the odd and the relevant. On the side of the merely odd, I should mention that Sir John Eccles, who received the Nobel Prize in physiology and medicine, in 1963, and who is, surely, one of the most informed students of brain physiology, drew together his philosophical speculations in a book based on a lifetime of specialized study and, turning as he was bound to do to the question of the relationship of cerebral activity to valid knowledge of the external world, resolved the matter in a single reference in accord with his memory of Dewey's views. The book was published in 1970, not a very long time ago; and in it, Eccles remarks that the question mentioned usually is considered in relation to visual perception. Perception, he says, "is assumed to be an inborn property of the nervous system. On the contrary, the visual world is an interpretation of retinal data, that has

117

been learned through association with information from sense organs, particularly those of muscles, joints, skin and the inner ear, and is the end-product of a long effort of progressive learning by trial and error." To this he adds: "cf. DEWEY, 1898"—that is, the third edition of Dewey's *Psychology*.[1] It is a curious tribute to Dewey that, in the impressively up-to-date bibliography that he provides, Eccles should have found the key to his solution of a very difficult matter in Dewey's very first book.

On the side of the oddly relevant, I should mention that the first John Dewey Lecturer, W. V. Quine, devotes at least one essay, in the book that collects the lectures and a bit more, to what he describes as naturalizing epistemology.[2] There he rejects the "old" epistemology, by which he appears to mean what is sometimes called foundation theory[3]—best illustrated perhaps by sense-data reduction (having Carnap in mind) or by epistemic dependence (in a more recent idiom) on self-intimating states.[4] "The old epistemology," he says, "aspired to contain, in a sense, natural science; it would construct it somehow from sense data. Epistemology in its new setting, conversely, is contained in natural science, as a chapter of psychology." Still, Quine finds a measure of validity in both strategies, as indeed he must, in order to remain consistent with the earlier views of *Word and Object* and his conception of the dogma of reductionism.[5] Hence, he adds: "We are studying how the human subject of our study posits bodies and projects his physics from his data, and we appreciate that our position in the world is just like his. Our very

118

epistemological enterprise, therefore, and the psychology wherein it is a component chapter, and the whole of natural science wherein psychology is a component book —all this is our own construction or projection from stimulations like those we were meting out to our epistemological subject. There is thus reciprocal containment, though containment in different senses: epistemology in natural science and natural science in epistemology."[6] Quine's view, then, is a decided improvement on Eccles', but its essential theme—both the pragmatism and the reliance on the role of retinal stimulation within a pragmatic theory—is extremely close to the view that Eccles summarizes from the *Psychology*. In effect, it is designed to permit only epistemologies that reject any and all forms of direct perceptual realism.

By a certain cunning of history—that is, by a selection of texts—our initial detour illuminates Dewey's own theory of knowledge. There is a certain deep weakness in the essential theme that Eccles and Quine share with what is reported as Dewey's view in the *Psychology*. It may be conveniently fixed in the context of Quine's theory of language learning and observational knowledge, though it has the widest possible consequences, for instance regarding the view that terms may be initially matched with their referents (as would be required by any form of sense-data reduction) and regarding the view that the sentences of one language, taken singly, can be translated into the sentences of another (as would be required by any advocacy of the analytic/synthetic distinction). The issue repays our close attention. Quine holds that "an observation sentence is one on which all

119

speakers of the language give the same verdict when given the same concurrent stimulation. To put the point negatively, an observation sentence is one that is not sensitive to differences in past experience within the speech community"; again, that "observation sentences are the sentences on which all members of the community will agree under uniform stimulation."[7] How do we determine membership in the same community? "Simply general fluency of dialogue."[8] In fact, Quine says that we can "always get an absolute standard by taking in all speakers of the language, *or most*."[9] The concession, prompted by the claim of Russell Hanson (and others) that observation is inherently theory-laden and sensitive, in Quine's own terms, to "differences in past experience" was designed to eliminate "occasional deviants such as the insane or the blind."[10] On Quine's own view, however, it would be difficult to sort the insane and the blind from those whose observation varies because of differences in past experience, because that would seem to mean that some set of observation sentences could be fixed relatively independently of the total theories of given speech communities, in virtue of which both meanings and referents of terms and the sensory foundations of scientific knowledge could be neutrally specified. In this sense, Quine is caught in a dilemma of his own making, for he is bound to avoid admitting any observations or observational sentences that would tend to yield a foundational view like that of Carnap's *Logische Aufbau*, and he is bound to insist that a speech community can be said to agree or concur or share the same verdict under the condition of being subject to the same concurrent stimulation or ocular irradiation or the like. The trouble is (it is the quintessential difficulty of Quine's philosophy) that there is an enormous conceptual gap between conceding shared *observations* and conceding, say, shared retinal *irradiation*. Not only is it doubtful that the same retinal exposure subtends the same observations or that the same observations subtend the same retinal data: constancy of sensory stimulation at nerve endings is not even the right kind of factor by which to fix the public and relatively constant perceptual world; the best that we can expect here is to theorize about the *constancy of information (itself controlled by a molar model of the life of a community of creatures) over changing sequences of external stimulation.*[11] Even to speak of consensus, therefore, is to invoke the body of concepts and beliefs of a community—*not* some allegedly neutral stimulations of sensory surfaces. But that, precisely, is to disallow the pertinence of similar external stimulation or, properly interpreted, the possibility of using it to fix the consensus of a speech community either with respect to the meanings of sentences or with respect to the truth of what is believed. This is in fact the key to the difficulty of Quine's generally behavioristic theories of language comprehension and perceptual cognition.[12]

The critical point, however, which returns us to the problem of epistemic realism is that, as far as language is concerned, word (or term) and sentence are conceptually linked in such a way that no sentences could even be specified without, at the same time, specifying (at least implicitly) the force of terms designating particular stimuli and particular responses; and as far as perception is concerned, that would-be external stimuli are perceptually relevant, that they are actually stimuli which prompt perceptual beliefs and cognitive assent, presupposes some reference to the conceptual scheme shared by a speech community in virtue of which, *derivatively*, our theories may come to the putatively neutral causal factors Quine favors. Notoriously, Quine avoids both concessions.[13] Thus Quine's formula: "*A* is epistemologically prior to *B* if *A* is causally nearer than *B* to the sensory receptors. Or, what is in some ways better, just talk explicitly in terms of causal proximity to sensory receptors and drop the talk of epistemological priority." Or, again, "observation sentences are sentences which, as we learn language, are most strongly conditioned to concurrent sensory stimulation rather than to stored collateral information."[14] The trouble, then, very simply put, is that there is no independent sense in which observation sentences *are* "causally closer" to sensory stimulation than other sentences also said to be observational but more heavily dependent on collateral information. This is the reason why epistemic realism, not necessarily naive (or naively direct) realism, is unavoidable. We can never expect to capture our knowledge of the external world if we begin with putatively external stimuli characterized without regard to our cognitive orientation and capacity, just as we cannot expect to do so if we begin with private sense data.

It happens, as history's cunning requires, that this view is especially congenial to Dewey's most mature—in effect, his comparatively late—reflections on the nature of knowledge. Dewey naturalizes epistemology, too. But he does so, in contrast to Quine's method, by invoking what he sometimes calls "the biological-anthropological method."[15] Now, Dewey's language is not always light or transparent, and a good many of his scattered and gradually refined views are either misleading or downright indefensible. But it is remarkable how similar and yet how dissimilar are Quine's and Dewey's accounts of the beginning of inquiry—and how crucial to the characterization of epistemology the similarities and differences are. In the very first lines of Quine's *Word and Object*, we find the following: "This familiar desk manifests its presence by resisting my pressures and by deflecting light to my eyes. Physical things generally, however remote, become known to us only through the effects which they help to induce at our sensory surfaces."[16] Recalling what has already been said, we see that Quine must have conflated a general naturalism about the acquisition of knowledge, that knowledge arises out of encounters between sensitive organisms and environing objects focused in an essential way on the irritation of our sensory surfaces, with a behavioristic theory of cognition fixed in terms of the irritation of those same surfaces; and since he reads behaviorism in a particularly strict way, allowing no Intentional or anthropomorphic or mental qualification in this second account (once canonically rendered), Quine is bound to construe external stimuli affecting the acquisition of language or perceptual knowledge as capable of being marked without reference at all to whatever we may suppose to be the biological orientation (including but not exhausted

123

by the cognitive orientation) of the creatures we are. This is essentially what Dewey rejects, which, in view of Quine's dilemma, promises more than an *explication de texte*. In any case, Quine is initially hampered by the radical behaviorist's avoidance of central functional states because, precisely, their admission is conceptually linked to linguistic intentions and the earliest possible entry of intersubjective agreement on denotation and reference.

Dewey's theory of language appears to be disappointing, also. Max Black finds that, apart from Dewey's somewhat thin acceptance of George Herbert Mead's concept of the "generalized other," Dewey's account is "marred by two large mistakes": the first, that "he treats the meanings of words and the meanings of sentences as if the two belonged to the same logical category"; the second, that although he "consciously rejected an identification of meaning with psychic events or transcendent essences . . . he seems to have been unaware of still conceiving of meanings as a *nonverbal counterpart* of a symbol."[17] Curiously, Quine's counterpart commitments appear to be that the meanings of sentences (at least what Quine calls "stimulus meanings") can be determined without regard to the meanings of words, and that such meanings may be construed in terms of nonverbal correlates of given speech utterances. Still, it is useful to emphasize the resilience of Dewey's philosophical program as opposed to his particular doctrines on language and knowledge—especially where his own errors are extremely close to those of other even more influential views, because the corrections required are fully compatible with Dewey's "biological-anthropological" method but are essentially incompatible with the claims of radical behaviorism.

Furthermore, neither Dewey nor Quine offers a fully articulated account of the grounds for justifying *particular* ascriptions of knowledge. The question has been brought home to us in a strenuous way by the appearance of the famous Gettier problem, which has shown how difficult it is to construe knowledge in terms of the classic formula of justified true belief.[18] Both Dewey and Quine seem fairly content to appeal to the available procedures of science, though this is hardly to resolve the conceptual puzzle about ascriptions of knowledge in particular contexts. The result is that both their accounts of the nature of knowledge strike us as extremely general and unsatisfactory. They do so because we anticipate a solution to the justificationist puzzle about knowledge, in terms of necessary and sufficient conditions; but should it prove impossible to satisfy that expectation in a compelling way, the very largeness and generality of their respective views will come to seem a virtue. Nevertheless, there is an important difference between the two which actually favors Dewey's account. And, as I hope to suggest, there are surprisingly many fundamental questions about epistemology that are illuminated by the contrast.

First of all, then, there is the notorious matter of the pragmatic theory of truth. The pragmatic thrust of Quine's own view, despite his demurrer, can hardly be misread in the following:

Scientific method is the way to truth, but it affords even in principle no unique definition of truth. Any so-called pragmatic definition of truth is doomed to failure equally. [But] there may be some consolation in the following [reflection]. If there were (contrary to what we just concluded) an unknown but unique best total systematization θ of science conformable to the past, present, and future nerve-hits of mankind, so that we might define the whole truth as that unknown θ, *still* we should not thereby have defined truth for actual, single sentences. We could not say, derivatively, that any single sentence S is true if it or a translation belongs to θ, for there is in general no sense in equating a sentence of a theory θ with a sentence S given apart from θ.[19]

Dewey's way of putting essentially the same point—for Quine and Dewey effectively agree here—is this (formulated against Bertrand Russell's objections):

There is a distinction made in my theory between validity and truth. The latter is defined, following Peirce, as the ideal limit of indefinitely continued inquiry. This definition is, of course, a definition of truth *as an abstract idea* . . . Apparently Mr. Russell takes the statement to apply *here and now* to determination of the truth or falsity of a given proposition —a matter which, in the sense of validity as just stated, is determined, on my theory, by a resolved situation as the consequence of distinctive operations of inquiry . . . The "truth" of any present proposition is, by the definition, subject to the outcome of continued inquiries; *its* "truth," if the word must be used, is provisional; as *near* the truth as inquiry has *as yet* come, a matter determined *not* by a guess at some future belief but the care and pains with which inquiry has been conducted up to the present time.[20]

There could hardly be any closer agreement, which not only defuses Russell's criticism of the pragmatic theory of truth (better directed against William James)[21] but also provides an excellent reason for supposing that the perfection of the justificationist theory of knowledge is misguided.[22] The clue is a simple one: on any justificationist theory, a necessary condition for ascribing to any agent knowledge that P, is that P is true; but to determine that P is true, we who make the ascription must know that P is true. Consequently, the problem of ascribing knowledge to any agent cannot, for conceptual reasons, be separated from a general theory of truth or the way in which human inquirers move to discover what is true. But if truth must be characterized in the way Quine and Dewey believe, it is a foregone conclusion that ascriptions of knowledge cannot but be informal and provisional. For what we must see in their caution is a recognition that *no* definition of truth (as opposed to an analysis of the peculiar predicate "true" or the provision of operational criteria for appraising particular truth claims) can possibly have any direct operational payoff. Correspondence and coherence theories of truth are no different in this regard; and Dewey and Quine simply link the characterization

127

of truth to the favored themes of their respective theories.

This very concession, however, draws us on to the difference between Dewey's and Quine's conception of the process of human inquiry. Both men are epistemological realists, but their views are troublesomely attenuated by the pressures of historical antecedents. Quine wishes to avoid particularly the foundational confidence of Carnap's *Aufbau*, that rests jointly on sense data and self-evident logical truths. And Dewey, somewhat more globally, wishes to avoid a whole host of apparent historical blunders—including, prominently, the direct realism and certainty of sense-datum theories, unknowable noumenal objects, and idealist constructions of reality. The Deweyan theme is rather nicely sounded in the following accommodation by a friendly author, though in a way that fixes rather than clarifies the essential puzzle: "The enduring truth of idealism is that factuality must be qualified by meanings before we can make judgments about it. The enduring truth of realism is that factuality must have a brute quality and articulate structure of its own before judgments can have relevance and validity. The enduring truth of pragmatism is that, as active organisms, we are in the world and of it, we don't altogether have to acquiesce in facts as they come, we can alter the facts as they affect us by operationally applying our purposes and meanings to them so that they become data for knowledge by becoming data for successful action."[23] What we have here is a useful statement of how the pragmatist views his own relationship to realism and idealism rather than of how he actually absorbs the contribution of those other two doctrines. This poses an especially strenuous difficulty for Dewey's account, but it is also curiously matched in Quine's.

Without a doubt, Dewey's theory of inquiry is the driving force of his entire philosophy. And yet, his account of inquiry has been generally viewed as baffling in its own right. Here is what he says: "Inquiry is the controlled or directed transformation of an indeterminate situation into one that is so determinate in its constituent distinctions and relations as to convert the elements of the original situation into a unified whole."[24] Dewey also says, with an eye to clarifying the nature of situations, which are said to have certain seemingly anthropomorphic traits, that

> the unsettled or indeterminate situation might have been called a *problematic* situation . . . The indeterminate situation becomes problematic in the very process of being subjected to inquiry. The indeterminate situation comes into existence from existential causes, just as does, say, the organic imbalance of hunger. There is nothing intellectual or cognitive in the existence of such situations, although they are the necessary condition of cognitive operations or inquiry. In themselves they are precognitive.[25]

The easy way to make sense of these remarks is to understand them as maneuvers within Dewey's peculiar idiom designed to link ordinary cognitive distinctions continuously with whatever more fundamental forces are at work, below the level of cognition, in the life of human beings as biologically sensitive and culturally formed creatures. If you run through all of Dewey's cognitive categories, you will find a certain tripartite equivocation on terms—admittedly an expensive luxury but not at all as confusing as his critics would have us believe.[26]

There is, first of all, the tendency to use terms, ordinarily reserved for cognitive contexts, in noncognitive ways; or, alternatively, to deform their usual cognitive sense in a way that accords with the fallibilism and provisional nature of inquiry intended by the pragmatic theory of truth. Thus, for instance, Dewey insists on a noncognitive sense of perception, associated with sensory information that contributes to animal survival and adjustment processed even below the level of awareness.[27] Correspondingly, he insists, in a rather Jamesian manner, that cognitive experience is dependent on, and included within a wider range of, noncognitive experience.[28] Again, Dewey deliberately alters the usual sense of "knowledge," holding not only that "we experience things as they really are apart from knowing" but also that "knowledge is a mode of experiencing things which facilitates control of objects for purposes of non-cognitive experiences";[29] or, alternatively, that "the true object of knowledge resides in the consequences of directed action."[30] By this maneuver, Dewey intends to oppose a purely spectator theory of knowledge, to incorporate the cognitive agent in a process of inquiry grounded, subcognitively, in a biological and cultural milieu. The liberties he has taken have seemed preposterous to some.[31] But perhaps a trimmer way of holding on to

Dewey's insight is simply to claim that, even in standard ascriptions of knowledge, one must presuppose a model of rationality, a functional model of the reasoning processes of the human being keyed to normal needs, wants, intentions, beliefs, and actions, in virtue of which alone particular ascriptions may be justifiably made.

This is an extremely important and subtle issue. The denial of the usual foundation theories—whether of directly perceived sense data (Carnap) or of indubitable "self-presenting" states (Chisholm)—entails, as has recently been argued by Gilbert Harman, that all "knowledge of the world is based on inference."[32] But in the absence of any straightforward procedure for examining the *structure* of the mind's processes (as, for instance, by some mind/brain identity theory), we are obliged to ascribe a certain *functional* system of reasoning to human beings in virtue of which would-be knowledge may be taken to involve the appropriate kind of reasoning. This is impossible to provide, however, without some theory of the functional organization of the biological and cultural life of man. Here, in a nutshell, is a dramatic clue to the advantage of Dewey's "biological-anthropological" method over Quine's radical behaviorism, because, as we have seen, Quine's conception of the stimulation of sensory nerve endings concedes nothing to the functional organization of the cognitive and noncognitive life of man. Also, if the functional account of reasoning were, in the context of ascriptions of knowledge, heuristically applied and if knowledge entailed reasoning, we should have a very strong basis for regarding the justificationist account of knowledge as wrongheaded.[33] Again, given the pragmatic theory of truth and Dewey's deliberate adjustment of the concept of knowledge (to bring it into accord with that theory and the fallibilist interpretation of inquiry), it suddenly becomes plausible why Dewey repeatedly insisted on replacing "knowledge" with "warranted assertibility." For by "warranted assertibility" Dewey wished to emphasize that what we come to believe is contextually warranted by the process of inquiry itself, that it cannot be specified as knowledge independently of that relation.[34] In terms of the improvement suggested, once again, ascriptions of knowledge presuppose the proper forms of reasoning functionally assigned to men in the setting of their natural life. Foundational theories would not, if valid, require the adjustment; spectator theories celebrate the unexplained achievement of knowledge itself; and radical behaviorism fails to reach as far as actual cognition.

There is another consequence. The theory of inquiry that Dewey espouses—perhaps all pragmatist versions of inquiry that realistically concede an external world but that treat the actual details of scientific knowledge as the precipitates of inquiry—yields a psychologism as well. It is true that Dewey takes the trouble to deny that the " 'foundations' [of logic] are psychological," but he clearly means this in the sense of denying that logic must rest on an antecedent account of "sensations, sense-data, ideas and thought, or mental faculties generally, as material that preconditions logic" (p. 21). But he is not and could not consistently be opposed to construing logic, which he characterizes as "inquiry into inquiry" (p. 20) as the study of the laws of reasoning.

He denies a basic difference between logic and methodology, and he treats logical forms as "intrinsically postulates of and for inquiry . . . conditions discovered in the course of inquiry itself, which further inquiries must satisfy if they are to yield warranted assertibility as a consequence" (p. 16). He treats postulates as stipulations and argues that the laws of logic are "neither arbitrary nor externally *a priori*"; they are, in fact, Dewey thinks, "empirically and temporally *a priori*" as regulating future inquiries—and in that sense subject in principle to revision (p. 17). But he is not opposed to logical necessity. He attempts, in a somewhat murky account, to distinguish between propositions concerned with "analyses of single meanings or conceptions" and "propositions about objects and traits . . . involved *with* one another *in* some interaction hav[ing] reference to the contingencies of existence": the first, he thinks, exhibit necessary relations; the second, only probabilities (pp. 85, 279). But he moderates the opposition (uncertainly it must be admitted), holding that "the internecine logical war between empiricists of the type of Mill and the school of rationalism will continue as long as adherents of the one school and of the other fail to recognize the strictly intermediate and functional nature of the two forms of propositions as cooperative phases of inquiry" (p. 280).[35]

There is, it may be noted, an extraordinary similarity between these views of Dewey's and the very recently expressed views of Harman's on inference—which is worth fixing. Harman openly espouses an explicit psychologism, that "the valid principles of inference are those principles in accordance with which the mind works." Harman adds, in a telltale phrase that would be disastrous outside of pragmatism, that "the relevant rules concern the working of the mind when nothing goes wrong: [when] it works ideally."[36] He also says, "the principles of inference are not even known . . . they cannot be clearly stated; and no statement of an inductive rule has the sort of certainty that attaches to the principles of deduction"[37] Harman's resolution of the difference is simply to deny that "deduction is a kind of inference in the same sense in which induction is inference," because, it would seem, deduction does not concern what "we may infer or accept as explanatory . . . given our antecedent beliefs."[38] Nevertheless, Harman elsewhere inclines, more characteristically, to the Quinean doctrine that "what our words mean depends on everything we believe, on all the assumptions we are making. [Hence] we take another to mean the same by his words as we do only if this does not lead to the conclusion that certain of his beliefs are radically different from our own." But in that case, as Harman properly concludes, the account "allows no room for a distinction between analytically true assumptions and others."[39] Quine had already drawn the bold conclusion, also within a pragmatist's account, that "for all its *a priori* reasonableness, a boundary between analytic and synthetic statements simply has not been drawn. That there is such a distinction to be drawn at all is an unempirical dogma of empiricists, a metaphysical article of faith."[40] Dewey, like Harman, leans uneasily in the direction of Quine's simpler psychologism. But that psychologism, taken seriously, confirms once again the inadequacy of a justificationist theory of knowledge and the inherent informality of ascriptions of knowledge or of warranted assertibility.

Interestingly, however, Dewey's philosophical instinct provides for a perceptual realism as well as for the discovered necessities of logical forms; Quine's impulse, on the other hand, reacting against the twin foundations of Carnap's *Aufbau*, drives perception back to surface stimulation, and the very fixity of logical laws—which, in principle, can no longer be sharply contrasted with physical laws—is, for the behaviorist, correspondingly threatened. It is, so to say, the depth within a conceptual system that logical laws will occupy, or their strategic centrality within any such system, which explains their conservatism. "Dropping a logical law," Quine says, "means a devastatingly widespread unfixing of truth values of contexts of the particles concerned [that is, "and," "all," etc.]."[41] But he sees no way of denying that they may be dropped. Here a vexed question arises. While it may be true that a logical law, in the sense of some canonically formulated notation, may be held or dropped in alternative schematizations of a body of science, it is not at all clear—and Quine does not address himself to the question directly—that the minimal constraints of deductive inference regarding the avoidance of contradiction can be correspondingly dropped. (The other side of the matter, of course, is whether they can be formulated.)[42] It must not be supposed, however, that Quine is not a realist in the somewhat attenuated sense pragmatists concede: so he says, in a well-known remark, "The quest of a simplest, clearest overall pattern of canonical notation is not to be distinguished from a quest of ultimate categories, a limning of the most general traits of reality. Nor let it be retorted that such constructions are conventional affairs not dictated by reality; for may not the same be said of physical theory? True, such is the nature of reality that one physical theory will get us around better than another; but similarly for canonical notations."[43] But, precisely in having rejected a full-blooded perceptual realism, in retreating to ocular irradiations, surface stimulations, and the like, Quine risks the linkage with reality that his own insistence requires and that Dewey has been so intent on preserving. It is true that Quine speaks of "degrees of observationality," of a "gradation of observationality," which suggests an explicit perceptual realism; but he himself counters the suggestion, remarking that "in behavioral terms, an occasion sentence may be said to be the more observational the more nearly its stimulus meanings for different speakers tend to coincide"[44]—which we have already seen fails to capture the notion of cognitive perception itself.

In any case, the reason for pressing the point is simply that Quine, now on his own grounds, has no more way to contrast observationality with the intrusion of collateral information than he will allow in defense of the analytic/synthetic distinction.[45] But he himself sees the need, as we have already noted, to preclude the extreme views of such commentators as Hanson and Feyerabend. *If*, however, our perceptual realism is grounded in nothing stronger than the similarity of surface irritations, it will be very difficult if not impossible to deny, as Feyerabend insists, that perceptual discourse and perceptual distinctions themselves are controlled by theories that may, in principle, share no relevant terms or concepts.[46] The upshot is that pragmatism, precisely because of its view on the nature of inquiry and truth, because of its emphasis on fallibilism and on the prospect of alternative conceptual schemes being generated by inquiry itself, cannot avoid a full-fledged perceptual realism, on pain of trailing off into mere vacuity and even incoherence. Quine, intent on repudiating Carnap's foundations, provides an insufficient basis for avoiding a radical and universal skepticism about the sharing of meanings and perceptions. He *means* to avoid it, but his behaviorism will not let him. And perceptual realism is all the more plausible and systematic, once sense-data theories are rejected, if it is embedded in a theory of the biological and cultural creature endowed with certain characteristic skills and dispositions.

I asserted earlier that there was a triple equivocation, in Dewey's philosophy, on the usual epistemic terms. The first tendency involves the use of such terms to designate noncognitive phenomena and to alter or deform familiar cognitive phenomena in accord with the pragmatic theory of inquiry, in particular, with the continuous, so-called instrumental use of ordinary knowledge for on-going practical and consummatory interests. The second simply provides for the standard use of cognitive terms, where what is designated is now understood to be set in the large context of inquiry and to function there as a certain particularly useful abstraction. The third has occasioned a great deal of philosophical sorting: it has to do with the ascription of cognitively pertinent predicates—memorably, "doubtful" and "puzzling"—to actual "situations"; hence, it appears to involve the ascription of anthropomorphic attributes to objective reality—or, alternatively, to constitute a form of idealism. Dewey, of course, is emphatic about the theories associated with the third use. There is no way to soften the blow. Thus he says that "it is of the very nature of the indeterminate situation which evokes inquiry to be *questionable;* or, in terms of actuality instead of potentiality, to be uncertain, unsettled, disturbed. The peculiar quality of what pervades the given materials, constituting them a situation, is not just uncertainty at large; it is a unique doubtfulness which makes that situation to be just and only the situation it is."[47] Should anyone still misunderstand him, Dewey concludes:

> It is the *situation* that has these traits. *We* are doubtful because the situation is inherently doubtful. Personal states of doubt that are not evoked by and are not relative to some existential situation are pathological . . . Consequently, situations that are disturbed and troubled, confused or obscure, cannot be straightened out, cleared up and put in order, by manipulation of our personal states of mind . . . The biological antecedent conditions of an unsettled situation are involved in that state of imbalance in organic-environmental interactions . . . Restoration of inte-

gration can be effected . . . only by operations which actually modify existing conditions, not by merely "mental" processes. It is, accordingly, a mistake to suppose that a situation is doubtful only in a "subjective" sense.[48]

It is easy to misunderstand Dewey here. If one takes the spectator view of cognition—that there is an objective, cognizable world and that we are the subjects of its cognition—then the terms that Dewey introduces ("doubtful," "indeterminate," and the rest) will have to be ascribed to the real objects of our cognition. Clearly, that won't do. But Dewey's entire plan is to displace that picture and instead, as we have seen, to introduce the notion of inquiry as an interaction of a special sort between a certain biologically organized creature and its organized environment, which itself depends on certain *precognitive interactions*. It is just a step to see that the puzzling attributes Dewey introduces are to be ascribed to objective "situations," where, by "situations," Dewey means whatever in the precognitive phase of man's interaction with his natural and cultural environment generates inquiry. Such situations, systems of interactions, are "troubled," "doubtful," "questionable," in the precise sense that needs, drives, habits of life functioning below the cognitive level are baffled in their smooth and relatively automatic functioning by the particular properties—whatever they may be—of the external world (including ourselves) that "evoke discordant responses," balk the quieting of drives, obscure the anticipation of outcomes, and the like.[49] In this regard, Dewey insists that "the word 'subject', if it is to be used at all, has the organism for its proper *designatum*. Hence it refers to an *agency of doing*, not to a knower, mind, consciousness or whatever."[50] If a term is needed, what Dewey has called "situations" is what, today, might well be called *ecological systems* or the fragments of such systems as, in context, generate particular inquiries. They are, essentially, *functional* systems characterized in terms, precisely, of modifiable ranges of *normal* forms of human response to environmental stimuli. This is why Dewey insists that situations are "existential."[51] Inquiry develops as the cognitively emergent way in which organisms, already functioning precognitively at least in terms of survival, enlarge the range of interaction with the environing world. The anthropomorphized properties of such situations are not and are not to be projected to the clarified objective world of science. But the existential world thus characterized is also objective, in the only sense worth pressing —namely, that the cognitive discoveries of man make no sense and cannot be specified apart from a theory of the functional organization of human life itself. Human values, also, Dewey will go on to say, ultimately depend on an appreciation of human situations, because they depend on the way in which human beings actually function. But more narrowly, in the context of epistemology, this otherwise expansive and somewhat impressionistic thesis contributes the important insight that ascriptions of belief and knowledge are simply unintelligible when separated from a theory of the characteristic skills, dispositions, interests, intentions, and enterprises of man. Thus the very ascription of perception entails the conceptual capacity of organisms to discriminate this from that; and there simply is no promising theory of conceptual capacities which is not essentially linked to the functional life of the organisms involved.[52] This shows us once again the implausible restrictions placed on the justificationist theory of knowledge as well as the excessive economy of Quine's alternative view of inquiry.

With these distinctions in mind, Dewey's view of the objects of scientific knowledge falls neatly into place. "What science does," he says, "is not to correct the thing of ordinary experience by substituting another thing but to *explain* the former"; again, "it is not just the thing as perceived but the thing as and when it is placed in an extensive ideational or theoretical context *within which it exercises a special office* that constitutes a distinctively physical scientific object."[53] In short, Dewey construes the objects of science as theoretical posits controlled, minimally, by the constraints of perceptual realism and the existentially emergent conditions of inquiry itself. There are, as far as I can see, no further limits that Dewey places on the development of an adequate scientific theory. The result is that, though perception must be conceptually informed, theory-laden in effect, perception is not merely subtended by theory, as Feyerabend seems to suggest; nor are "the things of ordinary common sense knowledge" and "the so-called 'conceptual' objects of science" the objects of "rival claimants for occupancy of the seat of 'real' knowing"[54] —as Wilfrid Sellars apparently holds. Sellars claims that

141

"the assertion that the micro-entities of physical theory really exist goes hand in hand with the assertion that *the macro-entities of the perceptible world do not really exist.*"[55] But the odd difficulty of Sellars' view is that whatever entities are postulated by our *explanans* are taken to preclude whatever entities are postulated by our *explanandum.* Sellars, then, has no way, in principle, by which to admit human beings as cognitive agents relying in large measure on their perceptual capacities *if,* by a feat of their very own science, they must deny the existence of "the macro-entities of the perceptible world"—including themselves! Dewey, on the other hand, though admittedly not sufficiently systematic or explicit in his ontology and philosophy of science, seems prepared to accommodate whatever the sciences may disclose, provided only that such accomplishments are seen as the special deposit of the inquiring creature caught even precognitively in his environing world. More pointedly, there seems to be no clear evidence that Dewey was ever prepared to oppose an instrumentalist theory of theoretically posited entities to a realist theory and then to favor the former exclusively. His habit of using key terms with multiple senses is confusing; but what he does, in speaking of the theoretical entities of physical science, what he does everywhere, is to provide at one and the same time an account of how distinctions are to be understood in the context of on-going inquiry and how they are to be understood as the privileged and strongest precipitates of inquiry itself. For, Dewey explicitly says: "unless conceptual [that is, scientific] subject-matter is interpreted solely and wholly on the ground of the function it performs in inquiry, [the] difference in dimensions between the conceptual and the existential creates a basic philosophical problem. For the only possible alternative interpretations are either the (highly unsatisfactory) view that the conceptions are mere devices of practical convenience, or that in some fashion or other they are descriptive of something actually existing in the material dealt with. From the standpoint of the *function* that conceptual subject-matters actually serve in inquiry, the problem does not need to be 'solved'; it simply does not exist."[56] Consequently, though his preoccupation with the instrumental function of the objects of science (within inquiry) dominates—and therefore misleads, he nowhere wishes to deny that such objects are, on the evidence of inquiry itself, real enough.[57] The special concerns of different aspects of our inquiry lead us to emphasize somewhat different features as real. Minimally, we fall back, Dewey seems to think, to the characterization of existential situations, so that even tertiary qualities are (perhaps misleadingly though not necessarily indefensibly) said to be real.[58] In general, our common-sense concern is most closely linked to "practical uses and concrete enjoyments."[59] But Dewey also insists that there is "no sharp dividing line between common sense and science"[60] and even that science "is a potential organ for *organizing* common sense in its dealing with its own subject-matter and problems"[61]—a theme we can now appreciate that he shares in a distinctive way with the somewhat inimical but not entirely unpragmatic views of Feyerabend, Sellars, and Quine. His instinct here is sounder, even if his grasp of the details of science itself is not. He is more convinced than they of the pluralistic sources of our conceptual schemes and more convinced of the need to tolerate whatever there may be—less anarchical than Feyerabend, less confident of progress through the choice of globally opposed alternatives than Sellars, less restrictive of the immediate situations of human inquiry than Quine.[62]

Finally, about the initial reference to Dewey's *Psychology*, Eccles was quite right in his report.[63] But that itself strongly suggests the extent to which Dewey attempted to reconstruct the theory of knowledge and the continuing freshness of the venture.

Notes

1. John C. Eccles, *Facing Reality* (Heidelberg, Springer-Verlag, 1970), pp. 48 f.; cf. p. 66.

2. W. V. Quine, "Epistemology Naturalized," *Ontological Relativity and Other Essays* (New York, Columbia University Press, 1969).

3. Cf. Keith Lehrer, *Knowledge* (Oxford, Clarendon Press, 1974), chaps. 4–6.

4. For instance, prominently in the theory of Roderick Chisholm, *Theory of Knowledge* (Englewood Cliffs, N.J., Prentice-Hall, 1966).

5. Cf. W. V. Quine, *Word and Object* (Cambridge, MIT Press, 1960), chaps. 1–2. "Two Dogmas of Empiricism," *From a Logical Point of View* (Cambridge, Harvard University Press, 1953).

6. "Epistemology Naturalized," p. 83.

7. Ibid., p. 87.

8. Ibid., p. 87.

9. Ibid., p. 88; italics added.

10. Ibid., p. 88, note 7. See N. R. Hanson, "Observation and Interpretation," in Sidney Morgenbesser, ed., *Philosophy of Science Today* (New York, Basic Books, 1966).

11. Cf., for instance, J. J. Gibson, *The Senses Considered as Perceptual Systems* (Boston, Houghton Mifflin, 1966), chap. 12.

12. See Noam Chomsky's review of Skinner, *Verbal Behavior*, in *Language*, 35 (1959), 26–58; and Joseph Margolis, "Behaviorism and Alien Languages," *Philosophia*, 3 (1973), 413–427.

13. *Word and Object*, chap. 2. Cf. Margolis, "Behaviorism and Alien Language." Also Charles Taylor, *The Explanation of Behavior* (London, Routledge and Kegan Paul, 1964).

14. "Epistemology Naturalized," p. 85.

15. John Dewey, "Experience, Knowledge and Value: A Rejoinder," in Paul Arthur Schilpp, ed., *The Philosophy of John Dewey* (New York, Tudor, 1939), p. 526.

16. *Word and Object*, p. 1.

17. Max Black, "Dewey's Philosophy of Language," repr. *Margins of Precision* (Ithaca, Cornell University Press, 1970), pp. 239–240. Black's references are chiefly to *Logic, Experience and Nature* and *The Quest for Certainty*.

18. The relevant literature has become enormous. Two convenient reviews, in terms of both primary sources and the most recent sense of the issue, are provided in Michael D. Roth and Leon Galis, eds., *Knowing* (Englewood Cliffs, Prentice-Hall, 1970), and Keith Lehrer, *Knowledge* (Oxford, Clarendon Press, 1974).

19. *Word and Object*, pp. 23–24.

20. "Experience, Knowledge and Value," pp. 572–573.

21. Cf. Bertrand Russell, "Dewey's New *Logic*," in Schilpp, *The Philosophy of John Dewey;* Bertrand Russell, "William James's Conception of Truth," in *Philosophical Essays* (London, Allen and Unwin, 1910); and William James, "Pragmatism's Conception of Truth," in *Pragmatism* (New York, Longmans, Green, 1907).

22. See Joseph Margolis, *Knowledge and Existence* (New York, Oxford, 1973), chap. 1. Also Margolis, "Alternative Strategies for the Analysis of Knowledge," *Canadian Journal of Philosophy*, 2 (1973), 461–469.

23. Donald A. Piatt, "Dewey's Logical Theory," in Schilpp, *The Philosophy of John Dewey*, p. 126.

24. John Dewey, *Logic. The Theory of Inquiry* (New York, Henry Holt, 1938), pp. 104 f; italics in original.

25. Ibid., pp. 105–107.

26. Cf. Arthur E. Murphy, "Dewey's Epistemology and Metaphysics," in Schilpp; and Bertrand Russell, "Dewey's New *Logic*," also in Schilpp.

27. *Logic*, p. 67.

28. John Dewey, *Experience and Nature*, 2nd ed. (La Salle, Ill., Open Court, 1929; repr. Dover Publications, 1958), pp. 23–24, esp. note 1, in the context of chap. 1.

29. John Dewey, *The Quest for Certainty* (New York, Minton, Balch, 1929), p. 98.

30. Ibid., p. 196.

31. Cf. Murphy and Russell (above, note 26).

32. Gilbert Harman, *Thought* (Princeton, Princeton University Press, 1973), pp. 20 f.

33. This is emphatically not to endorse Harman's theory of knowledge, which, ultimately, risks vacuity.

34. *Logic*, pp. 8–9. The following quotations are from this work.

35. See Ernest Nagel, *Sovereign Reason* (Glencoe, Free Press, 1954), chaps. 7–8. Also the interesting notes provided by Patrick Suppes, "Nagel's Lectures on Dewey's Logic," in Sidney Morgenbesser, Patrick Suppes, and Morton White, eds., *Philosophy, Science, and Method* (New York, St. Martin's Press, 1969).

36. *Thought*, pp. 18–19.

37. Ibid.

38. Ibid., pp. 157–158.

39. Ibid., pp. 13–14.

40. W. V. Quine, "Two Dogmas of Empiricism" (above, note 5), p. 37.

41. *Word and Object*, p. 60.

42. Cf. Ernest Nagel, "Logic without Ontology," repr. Herbert Feigl and Wilfrid Sellars, eds., *Readings in Philosophical Analysis* (New York, Appleton Century Crofts, 1949).

43. *Word and Object*, p. 161.

44. Ibid., pp. 42–43. See Joseph Margolis, "Quine on Observationality and Translation," *Foundations of Language*, 4 (1968), 128–138.

45. *Word and Object*, cf. secs. 9–10, 14.

46. Paul Feyerabend, "Materialism and the Mind-Body Problem," *Review of Metaphysics*, 17 (1963), 49–66. "Problems of Empiricism," in R. G. Colodny, ed., *Beyond the Edge of Certainty* (Englewood Cliffs, Prentice-Hall, 1965). See Hilary Putnam, "How Not to Talk about Meaning," in Robert S. Cohen and Marx W. Wartofsky, eds., *Boston Studies in the Philosophy of Science*, 2 (New York, Humanities Press, 1965); and Joseph Margolis, "Notes on Feyerabend and Hanson," in Michael Radner and Stephen Winokur, eds., *Analysis of Theories and Methods of Physics and Psychology*, Minnesota Studies in the Philosophy of Science, 4 (Minneapolis, University of Minnesota Press, 1970).

47. *Logic*, p. 105.

48. Ibid., pp. 105–106.

49. Ibid.

50. "Experience, Knowledge and Value," p. 542.

51. *Logic*, chap. 6.

52. See, e.g., Bede Rundle, *Perception, Sensation and Verification* (Oxford, Clarendon Press, 1972).

53. "Experience, Knowledge and Value," pp. 538–539.

54. Ibid., pp. 536–537. Also *Experience and Nature*, pp. 319–325.

55. Wilfrid Sellars, *Science, Perception and Reality* (London, Routledge and Kegan Paul, 1963), p. 96. See Joseph Margolis, "Some Ontological Policies," *Monist*, 53 (1969), 231–245.

56. *Logic*, p. 467.

57. As Ernest Nagel puts it: "there is no incompatibility between maintaining that scientific objects function as conceptual tools in inquiry, and holding that in addition they play a role as elements in the executive order of nature": *Sovereign Reason*, p. 114. Cf. Sidney Morgenbesser, "The Realist-Instrumentalist Controversy," in *Philosophy, Science, and Method*.

58. "Experience, Knowledge and Value," pp. 540–543. Cf. Hans Reichenbach, "Dewey's Theory of Science," in Schilpp, *The Philosophy of John Dewey*.

59. *Logic*, pp. 66,

60. Ibid., p. 71.

61. Ibid., p. 77.

62. See John Herman Randall, Jr., "Dewey's Interpretation of the History of Philosophy," in Schilpp.

63. See John Dewey, *Psychology*, 3rd rev. ed. (New York, Harper, 1891), chap. 5.

5

John Dewey and the Truth about Ethics

JAMES RACHELS

THE DEEPEST and most diffi-
cult philosophical question about ethics—at least, in that
part of the subject we call metaethics—is whether there
is such a thing as objective moral truth. Do our moral
judgments say anything about the world which is true or
false independently of our feelings and conventions? Or
is morality nothing more than a human invention, perhaps merely an expression of the way we feel about
things? There was a time, of course, when such questions
would not have occurred to people, or if they did occur,
when the answers would have seemed easy. Then, the
world was almost universally regarded as the product of
divine creation; and everything in it, including man, had
its proper place and function. Given such an outlook,
there was no problem about ethics: man's duties followed
naturally from his assigned place in the scheme of things,
from his nature and from his role as God's child. It is
difficult for us now to appreciate how pervasive this
attitude was, and how different the world looked to

149

those who had it. We are amazed, for example, to learn that Sir Isaac Newton believed his most enduring contribution to human thought would be his natural theology; he believed this even while doing the work in physics that would so transform our world-view that natural theology would no longer seem a respectable subject.

For those of us who do not view the world from a theological perspective, the status of ethics is more problematic. Let me describe, in a general way, what the problem is. First of all, we think that some things *really* are good, and others *really* are bad, in a way that does not depend on how we feel about them. Hitler's concentration camps really were evil, and anyone who thinks otherwise is simply wrong. Therefore we want a theory that will allow for the objectivity of ethics. The most obvious way to construct such a theory is to regard goodness and badness as (nonrelational) *properties* of actions, or states-of-affairs, on a par with other straightforward kinds of properties. Thus to say that the concentration camps were evil is to state a fact—the fact that the concentration camps had the property of being evil—in much the same way as it is stating a fact to say that people were killed in them. People were killed in those places, no matter what anyone thinks and no matter how anyone feels about it; similarly, on this view, those places were evil no matter what anyone thinks and no matter how anyone feels.

This view accommodates our intuitions about the objectivity of ethics, and it has been defended by such eminent philosophers as G. E. Moore. Nevertheless, there are strong reasons for doubting whether it is correct. One difficulty has to do with the ontology of the theory. It is hard to believe, while maintaining one's sense of reality, that goodness and badness are properties in any simple sense. Hume put his finger on the difficulty in a famous passage in the *Treatise:* do such "properties" really *exist?*

> Take any action allow'd to be vicious: Wilful murder, for instance. Examine it in all lights, and see if you can find that matter of fact, or real existence, which you call *vice.* In which-ever way you take it, you find only certain passions, motives, volitions, and thoughts. There is no other matter of fact in the case. The vice entirely escapes you, as long as you consider the object. You never can find it, till you turn your reflexion into your own breast, and find a sentiment of disapprobation, which arises in you, towards this action. Here is a matter of fact; but 'tis the object of feeling, not of reason.[1]

Another difficulty, also recognized by Hume, is connected with the action-guiding character of moral judgment. To say that an act would be evil is to say that it is *not to be done;* this is a necessary part of what such judgments mean. But if goodness and badness are simply properties of things, the intimate connection between moral judgment and action is lost. How can the fact that an action would have a certain property *necessarily* provide us with a reason for or against doing it? Why couldn't we be just as indifferent to this "property" as to any other? What do such "facts" have to do with us and our conduct?

Faced with these difficulties, we are pushed toward the opposite view: that our moral judgments merely express our feelings, and nothing more. This view does not require us to believe that actions or states-of-affairs have any special properties beyond those revealed by a cold scientific analysis of them; so it does not share the ontological problems of the Moorean doctrine. Furthermore, on this view the connection between moral judgment and action is clear: if, in saying that something is bad, we are expressing our opposition to it, there is no mystery about why such judgments dispose us to act in one way rather than another.

But the subjectivist view is just as hard to accept as the other one, for now we have given up all pretense of objectivity. It would seem that we could make *any* action or state-of-affairs (including, for example, concentration camps) good or bad simply by adopting the appropriate attitude toward it. And there are other familiar problems with this view: if, in saying that something is good, I am merely expressing my favorable attitude toward it, am I then *infallible* in my moral judgments, so long as I express my attitudes honestly? And if someone else says that the same thing is bad, and he is accurately expressing *his* attitudes, are we both right?

So we find ourselves in the dilemma which Dewey describes in his Gifford Lectures, torn between contrary theories, both of which seem somehow necessary, but neither of which seems true. As Dewey puts it,

> we oscillate between a theory that, in order to save the objectivity of values, isolates them from experience

and nature, and a theory that, in order to save their concrete and human significance, reduces them to mere statements about our own feelings. (*QC*, 263)[2]

How are we to proceed from here? There are a number of options available. Noncognitivists such as Stevenson have argued, in subtle and ingenious ways, that the view that moral judgments express attitudes can be freed from the difficulties mentioned above.[3] Another option is to try to work out a form of ethical naturalism which will do justice both to the objectivity of ethics and to its intimate connection with human feelings and conduct, insofar as it is possible to reconcile those two matters. Dewey's theory of ethics is in this latter naturalistic tradition.

Like many students, Dewey tended to accept the views of his teachers, and so as a young man he was very much influenced by the Hegelian Idealism then fashionable. Eventually he rejected idealism, but throughout his life he retained the idealist's suspicion of any attempt to understand phenomena apart from their connections and relations with other phenomena. For example, the positivist doctrine that the world consists of "atomic facts," each independent of all the others, was especially abhorrent to him. There is a charming story, told by Ernest Nagel, which points up this aspect of Dewey's thinking:

I remember one memorable occasion when the late Otto Neurath sought to interest Dewey in the Unity of Science movement, by having him contribute a monograph to the *Encyclopedia of Unified Science* which Neurath was then planning. I accompanied Neurath and Sidney Hook when they called on Dewey at his home; and Neurath was having obvious difficulty in obtaining Dewey's participation in the *Encyclopedia* venture. Dewey had one objection—there may have been others, but this is the only one I recall—to Neurath's invitation. The objection was that since the Logical Positivists subscribed to the belief in atomic facts or atomic propositions, and since Dewey did not think there are such things, he could not readily contribute to the *Encyclopedia*.

Now at this time Neurath spoke only broken English, and his attempts at explaining his version of Logical Positivism were not very successful. Those of us who knew Neurath will remember his elephantine sort of physique. When he realized that his attempts at explanation were getting him nowhere, he got up, raised his right hand as if he were taking an oath in a court of law (thereby almost filling Dewey's living room), and solemnly declared, "I *swear* we don't believe in atomic propositions." This pronouncement won the day for Neurath. Dewey agreed to write the monograph, and ended by saying, "Well, we ought to celebrate," and brought out the liquor and mixed a drink.[4]

And that is how the *Theory of Valuation* came to be written.

In that book Dewey emphasizes that we cannot hope to understand the nature of moral judgments apart from the contexts or situations in which they are made. They are made in situations in which "there is something the matter," in which there is some conflict or problem to be solved. What typically happens is this. We want or need something which does not exist in the present situation; or, we have some purpose or goal which cannot be attained without effort on our part. Therefore we have to make a decision, to act or not to act, and if we choose to act, we have to decide which course of action to adopt from among the available alternatives. Perhaps if we choose one course, which satisfies some of our interests, other interests will be frustrated. The question, then, is what to do, and the "valuation" provides the answer by singling out certain actions, but not others, as to-be-done.[5]

Because evaluative judgments have this practical function—they direct conduct—some philosophers have thought that they have a different kind of meaning from ordinary factual judgments. Stevenson, for example, held that insofar as sentences are distinctively ethical, they have *emotive* meaning, which is different from the cognitive meaning of ordinary factual assertions. Ethical sentences express but do not report one's attitudes, in much the same way as one expresses but does not report an attitude in saying "Alas!" Ethical sentences are also used to influence other people's behavior, much as the cry "Help!" is an attempt to influence other people's behavior. Neither of these sentences describes any state-of-affairs; they do not, primarily at least, convey information. Their meaning is rather to be understood in terms of the way they express attitudes or influence conduct. And the same goes for ethical sentences.

Dewey argued that all of this involves "a radical fallacy." First, it is a mistake to draw conclusions about the content or meaning of ethical sentences from facts about their use. Dewey agrees that "the *entire* use and function of ethical sentences is directive or 'practical'" (this is what distinguishes them from ordinary factual claims, which only sometimes have a directive function); however, he adds that "It is quite another thing to convert the difference in function and use into a differential component of the structure and contents of ethical sentences" (*ESML*, 285). Second, Dewey argues that a Stevensonian analysis does not work even for such utterances as "Alas!" and "Help!", for even these utterances have cognitive, verifiable contents:

> Take, for example, the case of a person calling "Fire!" or "Help!" There can be no doubt of the intent to influence the conduct of others in order to bring about certain consequences capable of observation and of statement in propositions. The expressions, taken in their observable context, say something of a complex character. When analyzed, what is said is (i) that there exists a situation that will have obnoxious consequences; (ii) that the person uttering the expressions is unable to cope with the situation; and (iii) that an improved situation is anticipated in case the assistance of others is obtained. All three of these matters are capable of being tested by empirical evidence, since they all refer to things that are observable. (*TV*, 12)

Is there any case in which "alas" has meaning apart from something that is of the nature of a calamity, a loss, a tragic event, or some cause or deed which is mourned? I imagine that when a reader sees the word "emotive," he is likely to think of events like anger, fear, hope, sympathy, and in thinking of them he thinks necessarily of other things—the things with which they are integrally connected. Only in this way can an event, whether a sigh or a word like "alas," have identifiable and recognizable "meaning." (*ESML*, 292)

There is both something right and something wrong in what Dewey says here. He is surely right to insist that, taken in context, utterances such as "Help!" do somehow convey the idea that certain sorts of facts are the case, and that if such facts do not obtain, the utterer is seriously misleading his audience. I think, however, that Dewey goes wrong when he tries to explain this by making it a part of the *content* of such utterances that they *say* such facts are the case. When someone shouts "Help!", he does not literally *say* that there is an obnoxious situation with which he cannot cope. Dewey does not want us to forget the importance of the total context in analyzing acts of communication; but in emphasizing this he seems to have blurred the valid distinction between the *meaning* of a bit of language and *what we may legitimately infer* from the fact that this bit of language has been used.

Nevertheless, I think Dewey is right in his main contention about ethical language—that ethical sentences may be cognitively meaningful even if their use or function is practical. For unlike such utterances as "Help!" or "Alas!", there is every reason to believe that ethical sentences are true-or-false. The problem is, if ethical sentences do have a content that is true-or-false, what is it?

We may approach this question by examining the distinction between what is desired and what is desirable. Dewey gives a naturalistic analysis of this distinction, according to which what is desirable is simply what we would desire as a result of an impartial, intelligent review of the relevant facts. Again, we must start with the context in which desires originally arise. We want something, or we have a need for something, in a situation in which that thing does not exist. Alternatively, there is something in the present situation to which we have an aversion. Thus we are motivated to take some sort of action. If we pause to deliberate—that is, if we pause to think intelligently about the conditions that gave rise to our desire, about the object of the desire, and about the likely consequences of pursuing it through various means—several things might happen. The original desire might persist, stronger than ever, or it might be modified; new desires and aversions might be formed relative to various alternative actions. The point is that deliberation modifies, changes, and reinforces our desires; and what we desire as a result of this process is, on Dewey's view, what is desirable.

The contrast referred to [between the desired and the desirable] is simply that between the object of a desire as it first presents itself (because of the existing mechanism of impulses and habits) and the object of desire which emerges as a revision of the first-appearing impulse, after the latter is critically judged in reference to the conditions which will decide the actual result. . . . It points to the difference between the operation and consequences of unexamined impulses and those of desires and interests that are the product of investigation of conditions and consequences. (*TV*, 31–32)

This is all pretty general, and Dewey is not very good about providing concrete examples. So I will provide one which I think captures the spirit of what Dewey is after. Let us consider the position a man is in when he first confronts the moral arguments for vegetarianism, which, I think, are much stronger than people usually realize.

Suppose someone enjoys eating meat, and it has never occurred to him to question the morality of this practice. His action follows the pattern of "the existing mechanism of impulses and habits." But then he reads something on the subject of factory farming,[6] and he is disturbed to learn that raising and slaughtering animals for meat involves making them suffer in various awful ways that he never suspected. Now he finds that two of his desires are in conflict: he wants to continue eating meat, but he doesn't want to participate in any practice that involves cruelty. A third desire is also involved, namely his desire to remain healthy: he had always believed, in a vague way, that meat-eating was necessary for his health. But now suppose he learns that this isn't so, that in fact a vegetarian diet is just as nutritious as one including meat. So it begins to appear to him that the *only* reason he has for eating meat, and so for supporting the cruelties, is that he likes the way the animals taste. To top it all off, he learns that a diet including meat is wasteful, because we have to feed the animals much more protein in grain form than we get back in the form of meat; so that, if we did not eat meat, there would be considerably more food to go around for the world's people.[7]

As a result of reflecting on all this, he might form a new set of attitudes toward meat-eating. He may find that his desires are not now what they were before. His old enjoyment of meat was, as Dewey puts it, one that "reflective judgments condemn" (QC, 263). If I understand Dewey correctly, an enjoyment that "reflective judgments condemn" is one that cannot be sustained in the face of knowledge and reflection; such enjoyments are unstable in the sense that they can exist only so long as one does not intelligently consider the relevant facts. The contrast is with likings and enjoyments that are reinforced or even produced by such reflection; these enjoyments "are not repented of; they generate no after-taste of bitterness" (QC, 267). If we picture a man whose desires are formed and sustained by his intelligence in this way, we have, I think, not only Dewey's picture of the good man, but also Plato's picture of the just man: his "passions" are under the direction of his "reason," and the parts of his soul are in harmony.

To return now to our question: If ethical sentences

have a content that is true-or-false, what exactly is this content? Dewey's answer, I think, can be expressed in this way: "X is desirable" means "X is such that it would be desired by someone who had considered, intelligently and without prejudice, the nature of X and its consequences." And although he is not explicit on this point, I think it is clear that he would define "X is good," "X is right," and "X ought to be done" in much the same way.

Dewey compares "desirable" with "edible," and I think the analogy is illuminating (*QC*, 266). Whether something is edible is a matter of fact; if something is not edible, we cannot simply decide to make it so by adopting a positive attitude toward it. Yet whether something is edible for us depends on the kind of creature we are as much as on the kind of thing it is. If we were different, what is edible for us might be different too. However, we would not say that a certain food was inedible simply because, for special reasons, it could not be eaten by a few people. We have a conception of what is normal for humans, given the kind of creature a human being is, and what is edible for humans is what may be eaten by the representative man, whether or not it can be eaten by every man. In the same way, the "someone" in my version of Dewey's definition of "desirable" may be understood as any typical, representative man.

It may be thought that the analogy with "edible" breaks down at a crucial point. "Edible" means, roughly, "*capable* of being eaten," whereas "desirable" (in the sense relevant to ethics) means, again roughly, "*worthy* of being desired." So it may be thought that Dewey's theory trades on a confusion between two senses of "desirable"—"capable of being desired" and "worthy of being desired." The charge is that he thinks he has defined the latter, ethically relevant, sense of "desirable," but really he has only given a definition of the former sense of the term, which is not relevant to ethics. But I think this charge is not well-founded. It is the essence of Dewey's view that to be worthy of being desired *is* to be capable of being desired, *under certain circumstances*—namely, the circumstances of intelligent thought and reflection. Perhaps this is not correct, but it certainly is not a *confusion* of the theory: it is the theory itself.

I want now to consider three questions about Dewey's view. First, it is an important fact about moral judgments that reasons may be given to support them. Does Dewey's sort of naturalistic view provide us with an adequate understanding of the nature of such reasons, and their relation to the judgments they support? Second, does this view provide an adequate understanding of the nature of ethical disagreement? And finally, does it commit the naturalistic fallacy?

(1) If I say that you ought to do something—for example, that you ought to stop eating meat—you can ask *why* you should do it, and if there is no reason, you may properly ignore my admonition and conclude that I am wrong. This suggests that there is an important connection between moral judgments and reasons. One test of the adequacy of ethical theories is their ability to explain this connection.

Stevenson's theory, for example, fails at just this point. On his view the proposition "You ought to stop eating meat," insofar as it is a distinctively ethical proposition, has no cognitive content; its meaning is simply its use in trying to get you to stop. Therefore, if I can get you to stop simply by telling you that you ought to, there is no need for me to give any reason why. And if you do demand reasons, then *anything* that will influence your conduct in the desired way will count as a reason. Stevenson says, "*Any* statement about *any* fact which *any* speaker considers likely to alter attitudes may be adduced as a reason for or against an ethical judgment."[8] Thus, if my telling you that grass is green would make you stop eating meat, then "Grass is green" would be a reason why meat-eating is wrong.

For Dewey the connection between reasons and the moral judgments they support is a logical one, and not merely the contingent one that Stevenson suggests. This does not mean that the reasons entail moral judgments in the way that the premises of a deductive argument entail its conclusion. Rather, it means that in order for a moral judgment to be true, there must be—*logically* must be—reasons in its support. "You ought to do X" does not itself state a reason for your doing X, but it implies that there are such reasons, and if there are none, the original proposition is false. Dewey says, "For in my opinion sentences about what *should* be done, chosen, etc., are sentences, propositions, judgments, *in the logical sense* of those words only as matter-of-fact grounds are presented in support of what is advised, urged, recommended to be done—that is, worthy of

163

being done on the basis of the factual evidence available" (*ESML*, 296). And not just any facts can be cited in support of "You ought to do X"; they must be facts *about the nature and consequences of X* which would influence the desires of someone who was being intelligent and reflective about X. Thus I might try to convince you that meat-eating is wrong by telling you about the "conditions and consequences" of meat-eating, but other means would be irrelevant to the ethical issue.

(2) Another test of the adequacy of ethical theories is their ability to elucidate the nature of ethical disagreement. If you and I disagree about whether meat-eating is wrong, exactly what are we disagreeing about? And is there any rational way to resolve our disagreement, and decide which of us is right?

On Stevenson's view, our disagreement is not a disagreement *about* anything at all; rather, it is a disagreement *in* attitude.[9] So our ethical disagreement will be resolved when we come to have the same attitude, no matter how much we still disagree over the facts of the matter. There is no difference, then, between my showing my view of the morality of meat-eating to be correct, and my persuading you, by any propagandistic or rhetorical means available, to share my attitude.

Dewey's theory, I think, permits a much more plausible understanding of ethical disagreement. Rather than assuming, when two people disagree, that the difference between them is simply in their attitudes, we may begin by asking whether they have exercised their intelligence and reflective abilities in the required way.

164

Dewey emphasizes that, when we form our judgments about right and wrong,

> If intelligent method is lacking, prejudice, the pressure of immediate circumstance, self-interest and class-interest, traditional customs, institutions of accidental historic origin, are *not* lacking, and they tend to take the place of intelligence. (*QC*, 265)

The point is that, in the absence of intelligent thought, there are lots of considerations that might explain why people disagree in their evaluations. Suppose a vegetarian is arguing with a meat-eater, and he (the vegetarian) is convinced that he is right, but he cannot persuade his opponent. Now of course, on Dewey's view, no one should ever be *so* convinced he is right that he is unwilling to reconsider his view; but suppose the vegetarian has reconsidered his view, again and again, and he is convinced more than ever that he is right. Now how might he explain his opponent's continued disagreement? There are a number of possibilities. Perhaps he is not fully acquainted with the relevant facts, for example the facts about how animals are treated on factory-farms. Or perhaps he has not adequately reflected on such facts as he does know: perhaps he has not considered, in an imaginative way, what it must be like to be treated in the way these animals are treated. Again, perhaps what Dewey calls "prejudice" or "class-interest" is influencing his judgment: it is easy not to take the animals' interests seriously, because we enjoy eating them so much; and besides, "they" are not "us." And, as Dewey notes, the pressure of custom and traditional institutions is always great: eating animals is such a familiar part of our lives that it is hard to take seriously the idea that it may be wrong.

The understanding of ethical disagreement which goes naturally with Dewey's view is this: if we could always exercise our intelligence to the fullest, we could always agree on evaluations; however, since various forces and interests do interfere with our being fully rational, we sometimes disagree, and when we do, the disagreement is explained by the operation of those nonrational forces.

Now it might be thought that this is much too optimistic, that it seriously underestimates the differences between people. Aren't some people so basically different from others, in their attitudes and outlooks on life, that they would continue to disagree even if they could exercise their rational powers to the fullest? Aren't there differences in attitude between people that are beyond the power of reason to resolve?

It is certainly possible that there should be such differences, and to the extent that there are, what is desirable for one person may not be desirable for all. (Just as what is edible for one *need not* be edible for all.) Thus Dewey's theory does allow for the possibility of a kind of last-ditch relativism. I think Dewey is right, however, to insist that we should never assume, as an explanation of actual disagreements, that people are simply different. We should always go on the assumption that actual disagreements are due instead to some failure of rationality, and that the disagreement is susceptible to rational settlement. We should make this assumption because, even though it is possible that people are so different that rational methods will not suffice to settle their disagreements, there is no good reason to think that there are such basic differences—or, if there are, they are rare, and must concern matters of relatively minor importance. The evolutionary history of *homo sapiens* has produced a species of beings that are so alike in their basic attitudes and needs that the application of intelligence should enable them to reach common decisions as to what is desirable with respect to the things that really matter. Dewey writes:

> Within the content of morals proper there are at least two forces making for stability. One is the psychological uniformity of human nature with respect to basic *needs*. However much men differ in other respects, they remain alike in requiring food, protection, sex-mates, recognition of some sort, companions, and need for constructive and manipulative activities, and so forth. The uniformity of these needs is at the basis of the exaggerated statements often made about the unchangeability of human nature; it is sufficient to ensure the constant recurrence, under change of form, of certain social patterns. In the second place, there are certain conditions which must be met in order that any form of human association may be maintained, whether it be simple or complex, low or high in the scale of cultures. Some degree of peace, order, and internal harmony must be secured if men are to live together at all. In consequence of these two factors of comparative invariance, the extreme statements

sometimes made about the relativity of morals cannot be maintained. (*AE*, 34–35)

Considering these and other important similarities between them, a common ethic for human beings, or *at least* for all those sharing one society, should not be regarded as an impossible ideal.

(3) Finally, since Dewey's ethical theory is naturalistic —that is, it assumes the existence of nothing more than the natural world, and defines value in terms of the operation of human interests and intelligence within that world—the question must be raised whether his theory commits "the naturalistic fallacy."[10]

"The naturalistic fallacy" is not a very happy name for the subject that phrase refers to, for it is not concerned solely with naturalism, and it does not refer to a fallacy. The phrase was coined by G. E. Moore, of course, who thought that "good" cannot be defined.[11] Since naturalistic theories, and others as well, do try to define "good," Moore thought that all these theories are mistaken. But this does not mean that all these theories commit a common fallacy—a fallacy is a formal error in reasoning, such as affirming the consequent, or hasty generalization—it only means that they are all mistaken.

The argument that Moore used in attempting to prove that all naturalistic theories (and some others as well) are mistaken is the "open question" argument. It goes like this. First, we note that any definition of "good" can be expressed in the following form:

D: "X is good" means "X has the property P."

Then, we formulate two questions as follows:

> A: X has P, but is it good?
> B: X has P, but does it have P?

Now, the open-question argument is simply this:

> If D is correct, then A and B have the same
> meaning.
> But A and B do not have the same meaning.
> _____
> Therefore, D is not correct.

And the reason why A and B do not have the same meaning is that A is an "open question" but B is not.

Can this type of argument be used to show that Dewey's naturalistic definition of value is incorrect? The issue comes down to whether the following is an open question:

> X is such that it would be desired by someone
> who had considered, intelligently and without
> prejudice, X's nature and consequences; but is X
> desirable?

I don't think this is an open question—or at the very least, it is not so obviously an open question that Moore's argument is decisive. For if we already know that the intelligent, impartial consideration of every fact about X would lead an unprejudiced, rational man to desire it, is there really room left for doubt as to its desirability? Any reason that could be given to show that X is *not* desirable would, by definition, have already been taken into account, and would have already been allowed to have whatever weight it can have for a rational man. It may

169

be, of course, that what considerations will have weight for a rational man is relative to man's nature; but that is all right, for the logical character of the concept of value may simply reflect this fact.

Notes

1. David Hume, *A Treatise of Human Nature* (London, 1740), Book 3, Part 1, Section 1.

2. I will refer to Dewey's works by the following abbreviations:

AE   "Anthropology and Ethics," in *The Social Sciences*, ed. W. Ogburn and A. Goldenweiser (Boston, Houghton Mifflin, 1927).

ESML   "Ethical Subject Matter and Language," *Journal of Philosophy*, 42 (1945), 701–712; repr. *Pragmatic Philosophy*, ed. A. Rorty (Garden City, L.I., Anchor Books, 1966).

QC   *The Quest for Certainty* (New York, Capricorn Books, 1960). First published in 1929.

TV   *Theory of Valuation* (Chicago, University of Chicago Press, 1939).

3. Charles L. Stevenson, *Facts and Values* (New Haven, Yale University Press, 1963), chap. 7.

4. Corliss Lamont, ed., *Dialogue on John Dewey* (New York, Horizon Press, 1959), pp. 11–12.

5. Here Dewey is on the side of Plato, Kant, and others who argued that moral notions are essentially conflict-notions—that is, notions we need only because we sometimes find ourselves in a special sort of quandary about what to do. "When things are going completely smoothly, desires do not arise, and there is no occasion to project ends-in-view, for 'going smoothly' signifies that there is no need for effort and struggle. There is no occasion to investigate what it would be better to have happen in the future, and hence no projection of an end-object" (*TV*, 33).

6. Perhaps Ruth Harrison's *Animal Machines* (London, Stuart, 1964).

7. Frances Moore Lappe's *Diet for a Small Planet* (New York, Ballentine, 1971) contains a lot of information on this point.

8. Charles L. Stevenson, *Ethics and Languages* (New Haven, Yale University Press, 1944), p. 114.

9. Stevenson, *Facts and Values*, chap. 1.

10. Kai Nielsen argues that Dewey does commit the naturalistic fallacy, in "Dewey's Conception of Philosophy," *Massachusetts Review*, 1 (1960), 110–134.

11. G. E. Moore, *Principia Ethica* (Cambridge, Cambridge University Press, 1903), chap. 1.

6

The School and Society: Reflections on John Dewey's Philosophy of Education

FREDERICK A. OLAFSON

THE PRESENT status of the educational thought of John Dewey is highly ambiguous. Although there has recently been a strong revival of interest in many of the characteristic concerns of the progressive education movement, of which Dewey was clearly the leading philosophical spokesman, it does not appear that Dewey himself is a figure of much interest to most contemporary educational reformers. It may be that he is too strongly identified in the minds of the latter with the very educational system which they are concerned to change in a fundamental way—a system which, it is often said, was significantly influenced by Dewey's own educational philosophy—and, if so, this fact may well be what stands in the way of recognition of a significant continuity between Dewey's work as a critic and reformer of the status quo of his own day and current reform efforts.

There are other reasons, too, why Dewey would not be very likely to strike many of our contemporaries as a very sympathetic figure. His were not the qualities of mind or character on which such a high value has recently been set, and you will look a long time in the barren avenues of Dewey's prose without finding anything that even remotely suggests the spontaneity and panache that have become the accepted signs of authentic individuality. This is not to say that real and important strengths do not manifest themselves beneath the gray surface of that prose, and most notably a tenacity and sobriety of mind that have perhaps become too rare in our own day. But it is also a fact that Dewey's way of expressing himself is too often dishearteningly similar to the kind of institutional prose favored by many of his epigones—a prose that seems to proceed on its own level of abstraction and amid a singular paucity of concrete illustrations of what a given thesis comes to in the educational contexts to which it evidently refers.

If for no other reason than this, Dewey must strike many today as a quintessentially "establishment" figure, and as the almost official ideologist of the very system of educational practice that has recently been under attack. Then, too, Dewey took a very positive view of science; and although what he says about it often seems hard to connect with the way theoretical science actually goes about its business, the very fact that Dewey urged that the self-understanding of society should somehow be derived from a generalization of scientific method could hardly appeal to a generation grown wary of both the social benefits attributed to science and technology and the kind of human engineering that has in fact been the most visible extension of scientific methods into the area of human relationships. Finally, the whole contemporary penchant for extreme situations, for violence and for the exploration of the boundaries of sensibility and even sanity, would have been utterly alien to Dewey; and his life-style, in turn, would have seemed hopelessly bourgeois and stodgy to the age of the radical-liberal school person.

So much for the gross and obvious though not necessarily superficial contrasts that may account for the absence of any strong sense of retrospective affinity with Dewey's concerns. Perhaps if one were to compare him with some of his predecessors in the long line of exponents of what has come to be called "child-centered" education—with a Jean-Jacques Rousseau, for example— the differences of temperament and of personal and intellectual style would be no less great; and this fact should, it seems to me, alert us to the possibility that these differences may hide deeper affinities and continuities. Indeed I am convinced that such affinities are not only possible but real; and in this paper I want to identify and explore a major area in which the convergence of Dewey's thought with that of more recent educational thinkers seems unmistakable. The theme I have in mind is the relationship between the school and society; and the disposition which I believe to be common to Dewey and our contemporaries is a disposition to make this relationship central to all thinking about education and to understand the school primarily in terms of its characteristics as a social institution, as well as the degree to which these reflect, whether positively or negatively, the ethos of the society it serves. One difficulty in the way of any attempt to raise questions as to the fruitfulness of this approach is that the coupling of these two terms —"the school" and "society"—is now so well established as to be very nearly a cliché; this is simply to say that for most of us it reflects only the plainest common-sense approach to education. What, after all, could be more transparently appropriate than to insist upon a need for a congruence between the democratic character of a society as a whole and the democratic character of the schools of that society? This is, of course, just one example, although certainly an important one, of the forms in which a concern with the relationship of the school to society may manifest itself; and it, too, will very likely strike most people today as self-evidently true. I think I should say at once, however, that I do not share this sense of the transparent validity of the approach to educational issues that is reflected in the slogans I have cited, and in exploring Dewey's formulation of that approach my intention will be to make both it and the implications it carries with it appear a good deal more problematic. At the same time, I do not intend to deny that the social and even the political dimension of education has great importance and deserves close analysis in any serious philosophical consideration of education; and indeed one of my criticisms of both Dewey and our contemporary progressivists would be that they do not provide a satisfactory analysis of this important, though not all-important, aspect of education.

Before returning to the task, I want to draw attention to another dimension of this whole matter: the relationship of the conceptions of education which I will be discussing to the processes of social change that have been occurring in our society, both in Dewey's time and in our own. I am referring to the immense expansion of the American public school system during the early years of this century, and to the admission of a very much larger fraction of the total school-age population to those schools, especially at the secondary level. This new and greatly enlarged constituency which the schools have had to serve has inevitably exerted great pressure on the curricula and standards of these schools, which had previously served a much smaller and more homogeneous social group. In many ways, the situation created by these changes was like the one created in institutions of higher education after the Second World War, when something like mass higher education—something that no one had seriously thought of until quite recently—began to be a reality; and in both cases there was a manifest need for a body of thought that would justify the changes that inevitably came with expansion and the demands that were being made for still more extensive measures of accommodation of academic traditions to the needs and capabilities of these new constituencies.

I would not want to be understood as implying that the ideas of educational reformers then or now were somehow cynically worked up to rationalize changes that were going ahead anyway. Undoubtedly, a thinker like Dewey intended to legitimize only what he thought was valid and desirable in the process of transformation of the schools that was going on; and what he offered was, therefore, an interpretation of that process which was also to serve as a guide to its further development.

But if thinkers interpret the processes of social change which they seek to influence, there is also a sense in which those processes themselves may be said to interpret the thought of the philosopher or reformer. By that I mean that to the extent that an espousal or endorsement by a philosopher of some movement or process is not carefully hedged about with the kind of qualifications and conditions that enable one to say with a fair degree of specificity just what it is that this endorsement encompasses, one can hardly help interpreting some of the central ideas in the theory in the light of the system of educational practice with which they have been associated. This is not to deny that the deeper motivation of the philosophy and of the movement may be quite different; indeed, I am insisting that this in fact has been the case. What I want to draw attention to is the peculiar form of symbiosis that characterizes the relationship between these often disparately motivated entities and the way in which these quite different forms of motivation seem to converge, so that the one offers support to the other because certain potential areas of conflict between them are left unexplored. It is my belief that this phenomenon is observable at many points in the history of social thought, and that when it occurs one can fairly impute to the theory or doctrine that allows these ambiguities to persist a measure of solidarity with the features of institutional practice which it allows to stand without challenge as interpretations of its own theses. I also want to argue that this kind of detrimental convergence between critical thought and social actuality —the kind of convergence that can transform the former into an ideology—has characterized the tradition of liberal thought in matters of education. In the thought of John Dewey the tendency of which I speak is most visible in his treatment of certain characteristics which the school is to realize in itself in order to achieve a congruence with the democratic character of its parent society and the experimental character of scientific inquiry. The whole theme of the school and society, so fundamental in Dewey's thought, generates, I will argue, a series of implicit assumptions that were to be applied to institutions of higher education by the educational rebels of the 1960's, and once again in that peculiar mode of symbiosis with independent forms of motivation which was also characteristic of Dewey's relationship to the earlier movement of reform in the lower schools.

Dewey's concern with the social dimension of education is rooted in some of the deepest assumptions that underlie his philosophy as a whole. Much of what he says about the social character of experience and inquiry is cast in the form of a critique of certain assumptions that he believed to be characteristic of both our intellectual and social traditions. The fundamental vice of these established ways of thought to which Dewey returned again and again was their tendency to generate insuperable dualities in one area of experience after another, and thus to fail to do justice at the level of either theory or practice to the wholeness of that experience and to the relative and conditional character of all the distinctions we effect within it. When thought is interpreted as a contemplative activity addressing

itself to an essentially static kind of truth, action becomes the mere execution of directives deriving from
such contemplative activity and has no prospect of ever
contributing to or correcting the guiding conception of
the goals it is to produce. Such a conception of knowledge and its relationship to action is, Dewey tells us,
reflected in a corresponding organization of society into
classes, one of which has the executive authority that
derives from its ability to understand and enjoy the
ultimate goals to which social activity is to be directed,
while the other and lower class carries out the directives
of the upper without any real understanding of or participation in the consummatory experiences in which
the whole life of the society finds its justification. This
ordering of the intellectual and social worlds in turn
generates a corresponding conception of education in
which all the same dualities are preserved and reinforced.
Knowledge is understood as something preexistent and
static; and its authority is not subject to challenge or to
any real critical assessment. As a result, the school
charged with the imparting of knowledge conceived in
this way becomes necessarily authoritarian in character,
and its social complexion can hardly be other than conservative.

In its positive formulations Dewey's own theory of
experience and inquiry is designed to ensure that knowledge and action are not isolated from one another
through false intellectual or social dichotomies. To
begin with, both "experience" and "inquiry" are to be
understood in a sense that strongly emphasizes their
practical character and their direct implication in the

processes that go forward in our natural and human environments; they are not in any primary sense contemplative, nor do they address themselves to essences that maintain their stability through some form of ontological independence from the flux of natural existence. Knowledge is tied to action and in fact is itself a form of action; and inquiry is the process of devising and testing new meanings that natural situations may assume for us and new networks of interrelationship through which action may be intelligently guided.

— The need for such inquiry arises at those points in our experience—that is, in our intelligent commerce with our environment—at which indeterminacies occur and there is at least a temporary failure of that connectedness and continuity which enable a need or an impulse to assume the form of an effective and realistic action in a public milieu rather than in that of imagination or fantasy. As so qualified, inquiry involves the establishment of the objective validity of a schema of adaptive behavior, and this is to say its common or public validity. Inquiry thus offers its tentative conclusions for general evaluation, and it is accepted that the milieu of experience in which this evaluation is to be carried out is that of everyman. In this sense, the method of inquiry and of science generally may be said to be democratic, and it admits none of those restrictive devices that confine the apprehension of the true or the real to some elite fraction of humanity. The consciousness before which the credentials of any epistemic or moral claim must approve itself is thus a social consciousness—a social consciousness that is realized through free exchange and communication and through the critical evaluation of the products of individual intuition and inspiration.

It should scarcely be necessary to draw attention to the strong emphasis that Dewey's interpretation of experience and inquiry places on the fluid and changing character of human adaptation to its situation within its natural milieu. The great enemies of intelligence are rigidity and all those associated mental habits which maintain hard and fast distinctions in the face of an infinitely various experience. Insofar as Dewey's position simply expresses an antidogmatic stand which insists that the authority of tradition is never enough to establish the credentials of an article of scientific or moral belief and requires that beliefs and hypotheses of all kinds submit to a process of testing for which in principle any human consciousness can provide a suitable milieu, there is nothing to be said against it and a great deal to be said for it.

There remains, nevertheless, a certain ambiguity in the characterization of the logic of empirical science as social, especially when it is intended that this characterization should serve as the basis for an analogy between the democratic principle of social organization and the experimental method of science. This ambiguity results from the failure of the term "social" to bring out a very important feature of the scientific method by which the accreditation of "experiences" as bearing negatively or positively on the evaluation of some theory is governed. The point here is that while no human being's experience can be disqualified in principle from playing a role in the testing of a theory, whether on grounds of inherent

181

mental inferiority or by some other a priori criterion (and science is therefore in this sense universalistic or, if one likes, democratic), it does not follow that science is consensual in any sense that is at all close to the one that applies to democratic decision-making. Unless it can be ascertained that the observations or calculations that have been carried out by a particular inquirer are in fact the ones that are required by the internal logic of the theory under test together with other accepted canons of scientific procedure, the observations in question will simply have no scientific standing at all. In other words, while the milieu within which scientific theories have to be confirmed and disconfirmed is indeed public and excludes no one's experience a priori, it is just as important a fact that observations and experiments have to be qualified on the basis of the understanding they manifest of the perhaps very intricate theories on which they are to have a bearing.

It can thus be said that although observations have a vital role in confirming and disconfirming theories in sciences, these theories also lay down the conditions that have to be met by the observations; and there does not seem to me to be any parallel to this in the case of democratic decision-making. It is also a fact that the moment we leave the area of shared common-sense beliefs and use more demanding criteria of evaluation for knowledge-claims of whatever kind, a distinction does open up between the usually small group of persons who have mastered the use of these criteria and whose views therefore are accorded standing, and, on the other hand, the much larger group of persons who simply are not in a position to participate. The locus of such formations is typically an area in which a special symbolic code—a technical language of some kind—has developed; and it is the mastery of this language which defines the insider.

I have pursued this point at some length because I think it will prove to be of considerable importance in coming to terms with Dewey's notion of a society that is committed to the dual and related principles of democracy and scientific method. There is a noticeable tendency on Dewey's part to develop the thesis that associates these principles with one another in terms of a level of inquiry that is pretty much that of common sense—the level at which almost anyone can institute the observations and the rather modest experimental procedures that may be required and at which the class of members of a nonspecialist human society and the class of qualified inquirers virtually coincides. The rather simplistic paradigm of intelligent adaptation and co-operative behavior which Dewey develops at this level is intended to express the essentials of the procedures involved in both the scientific investigation of nature and the definition and regulation of the social inter-relationships of those who jointly pursue those inquiries. Experience at a common-sense level is thus represented as generating the higher-order concepts and norms by which both inquiry and society are to be governed; and the norms proper to free scientific activity are held to be congruent with and supportive of the norms governing a democratic society. But if this picture of the capacity of experience at a common-sense level for generating the norms by which both scientific inquiry and social life are to be regulated should turn out to be inadequate, we could expect a theory of education that is based on it to share these inadequacies. Specifically, one would be compelled to wonder whether such a conception of education could do justice to those aspects of social and scientific practice that resist assimilation to Dewey's paradigm of an experience that generates its own norms. In what follows I will be arguing that this paradigm suggests a much smoother continuity than can in fact be shown to obtain in either domain and as a result -abstracts much too freely in one and the other case from the fact of our dependence upon "preexistent knowledge" and cultural tradition.

I turn now to Dewey's theory of education itself, and begin by noting that almost from the start his interpretation of the social function of the school labors under a severe internal tension. On the one hand, the school is designated as the instrument by which a human society transmits from generation to generation the corpus of accumulated knowledge and skills for which the more informal and older methods of transmission through direct participation in the work and life of the community are no longer adequate. In this respect, the school serves the social purpose of initiating the members of a society by enabling them to acquire the various forms of competence which life in that society requires. Dewey, by contrast with some more recent educational thinkers, does not appear to entertain any doubts that there is indeed a valuable legacy of knowledge and culture to be transmitted, and he makes it clear that the teacher's function is to enable his students to reach the point where he already is. But at the same time Dewey is just as clearly not satisfied with any conception of the school as a stage of preparation and self-qualification for a life that is to come later; and he insists that a school is itself a major life-context, an institutional reality, and that as such it must exemplify and participate in the wider life of a democratic society. Underlying this insistence on the quality of experience and of social life which the school itself affords, there is a strong conviction on Dewey's part that the school congenitally tends to close itself off from the matrix of shared social life and to constitute an artificial world of its own in which a ritual and almost fetishistic status is accorded to certain accomplishments that stand in no readily definable relationship to the dominant concerns of the wider social life. In this connection it is particularly interesting that Dewey understands this isolation of the school from the life of its circumambient society as reflecting an overly individualistic way of conceiving the business of education as though it were entirely a transaction between the student and his teacher, the latter representing the subject matter which the former is to master. In a real sense, the deep purpose of Dewey's philosophy of education may be said to be the infusion of social meaning and relevance into the learning activity that takes place in the school and the replacement of the individualistic and intellectualistic organization of these activities by the style of cooperative inquiry which he held to be at the heart of democratic social practice.

The school was thus to be the pioneering example of a society whose business is inquiry and whose mode of inquiry is uniquely congruent with its democratic character.

If this was Dewey's aspiration for the schools (as, of course, it was for the wider society as well), he was just as deeply aware that the academic mind almost instinctively rejects it. The school was, in fact, in Dewey's view, an institution that had conspicuously failed to come to terms with its mission in a democratic society and which persisted in a conception of its task that isolated knowledge from practice and the life of the school from the concerns of the wider society. More importantly, it is to this firmly established attitude on the part of academic people that Dewey seems to attribute their failure to engage the interest of a large part of their constituency. Indeed, when one reads Dewey and encounters one statement after another that carries the plain implication that schools are remote and boring places, one can hardly help wondering for whom he is speaking and what experience of schools and education it is that he is presupposing. It is astonishing how few references there are in his writings to the sheer pleasure that learning can afford. The perspective seems all too often to be that of someone who feels no such pleasure in learning as such and who is as a result baffled and antagonized by the whole experience of finding himself in such an alien milieu. No doubt the rejoinder could be that this has indeed been the experience of countless students at all levels of education and that it is Dewey's great merit to have recognized this negative response to schooling, to have taken it seriously and asked how the school can improve its own performance, which is presumptively responsible for that response. Perhaps it is indeed just this immemorial resistance that the human species has offered to the constraints associated with organized instruction that finds its voice in Dewey's indictment of the schools; but it seems certain that it also reflects the special difficulties in assimilation to the culture of the school which arose when mass compulsory education was establishing itself and the schools were full of students who in another age would never have been asked to submit to these constraints. Viewed in this perspective, Dewey's philosophy of education assumes a special significance as an interpretation of the situation arising out of this unprecedented change in the social scope of the educational enterprise and as a set of directives for a reorientation of educational prac-tice that would be responsive to this new situation. What is perhaps most striking about this interpretation Dewey proposes of the difficulties under which schools were laboring is its essentially hopeful and optimistic assessment of the sources of the resistance with which they had to deal and of the positive contribution it could make to the renovation of instructional practice. But whether this optimism was realistic and founded on an accurate appreciation of the situation in the schools is, I suggest, an open question.

Very roughly, the proposal Dewey made was that instruction should be organized around the various socially important forms of human work which were to supply the context within which virtually the whole of human culture and knowledge could be made to take on a significant relationship to the lives of students. The supposition here is that students come to the school from this wider social world of which they have already at least a rudimentary understanding and in which they may even have an incipient place and function and then find that what the school offers has no visible bearing on the business of this world from which they come and to which after all they are to return. If, instead, the school treated the various categories of social work as the foci around which its own work were organized, a continuity would emerge between the school and society, and the alienating and purposeless character of "school work" would yield to a mutually enhancing contribution by the school at both the collective and the individual level. As it turns out, however, the examples Dewey gives of the ways in which social work could be used as a framework of instruction tend to be drawn from the simple stages of social organization at which the nature of the social world can be understood without any very substantial background of scientific or technical knowledge, and these simple stages were presumably chosen because they are suitable to the level of ability and interest of the quite young children whom Dewey presumably has in mind.

There is clearly a more abstract consideration at work as well, however, and this has to do with the fact that the general paradigm of a self-ordering experience with which Dewey is working finds a more plausible application at the level of simple social work than it would elsewhere. In the context of such work, involving as it does only goals that are already familiar and straight-forward ends-means relationships, it is doubtless possible even for younger children to effect a relationship to their natural milieu that involves a kind of experimentation as well as a learning from the outcomes of that experimentation and a resulting reconstruction of the situation in which these processes take place. It is a different question, however, whether such examples of adaptive behavior within a situation that can be adequately dealt with by the resources of common sense—that is, by resources that one can assume are already available—can serve as a useful model for learning generally, and especially for the kind of learning that effects a replacement of common-sense descriptions of certain elements in our experience by technical concepts which will permit us to ask and to answer a quite different order of questions about what is taking place in our world. The picture Dewey suggests of the connection between the interests of the child and the work of the school is one of a smooth continuity in which the relationships the child has already established with his natural and social environment are utilized for the purpose of leading him on to the more complex and remote conditions upon which the outcomes with which it is concerned depend. Obviously such interests do exist, and any teacher should try to capitalize on them. But the point that needs making and that never seems to emerge clearly in what Dewey says about these matters is that interests do not naturally address themselves to those aspects of a given subject matter that are significant for the purposes of understanding. Here rather clearly Dewey's favorite examples are at fault, drawn as they are, for the most part, from the manual arts or from subjects like history and geography, in which the growth of knowledge can be represented as a pushing-out of the life-perimeter of the child in space and time. Even that can involve difficulties, but what is more important is that it is so often necessary to divert the child's attention from the features of a situation to which his interests naturally address themselves and to concentrate attention on matters that are in fact remote from these interests.

Perhaps if Dewey had used as his example of useful social work something like medicine, the point I am insisting on here would have received the emphasis it needs. Medicine connects at many points with the fact of health and illness with which we are all familiar, and it seems safe to say that even without schooling, our interests would attach themselves to these themes of our common experience. But if we are to understand medicine as a form of social work, we have to move beyond common-sense notions and the interests that define themselves in terms of such notions and learn the quite different language of medicine itself. In other words, here is a form of social work that incorporates a distinctive conceptual ordering of the phenomena with which it deals, one which we do not reach through any spontaneous pursuit of the pretheoretical interests we bring to our studies from our wider social experience. Here is "pre-existing knowledge" with a vengeance, and it involves a series of conceptual jumps rather than the kind of continuity of experiential process that Dewey regards as the norm for learning.

Medicine is, of course, not the only form of study which involves the conceptual discontinuities with our ordinary experience that I have been describing; and I would venture to say that every serious form of study—the kind for which organized instruction usually has been thought necessary—would reveal comparable features on examination. The issue this fact raises for a theory like Dewey's is simply to determine what distinctive force many of his theses about learning and inquiry retain once it is grasped that these processes involve a movement to conceptual levels other than those of common sense, and that conceptions of the social and experiential character of knowledge that are drawn from the sphere of common sense may prove highly misleading when applied to them. There is, of course, as I have already pointed out, a community of inquirers, and within it inquiry has some features in common with the democratic method, at least in the minimal sense I outlined earlier. A student may gradually qualify himself as a member of such a community and thereby become capable of generating the kind of "experiences" which may indeed test whatever theories he may be concerned with. But to suggest that in the process of such self-qualification—that is, in the process of education—there is in any meaningful sense the kind of continuity between experience and theory which would permit the one to serve as the test of the other is to foster an illusion. It is one thing to object, as Dewey does, to the various metaphysical interpretations that have been proposed of the preexistent character of knowledge; but it is another to press these criticisms

191

so far as to deny that knowledge as represented by the established disciplines of inquiry is preexistent for each individual child and student who seeks to qualify himself. There is, in fact, an unavoidable sense in which education is a matter of introducing students to something that is already known and that they would not have been able to work out for themselves within the model of self-evaluating experience which Dewey proposed. In other words, the school and the teacher are to make it possible for the learner to take advantage of someone else's past achievement and thus to move to a conceptual level at which the problematic features of common-sense experience may, to be sure, reappear but do so in a context of interpretation that may alter their significance and set them in a different perspective of action and control. In this sense what education has to offer is necessarily drawn from the accumulated corpus of discoveries, insights, and inventions that mark the historical points at which decisive steps beyond our common-sense understanding of the world were taken; and this corpus is the distinctively human legacy to succeeding generations.

In all of the foregoing I have been neglecting a major feature of Dewey's conception of the organization of education around the various important forms of social work; and this is its critical and reconstructive aspect. The codes defining the procedures by which such work is to be executed must not, according to Dewey, be thought of as a fixed canon which the student is simply to assimilate so as to be able to qualify himself as a participant in such work. Such a static picture of the nature of social work would remove it as effectively from the sphere of experience and process as would the various metaphysical ways of conceiving knowledge which Dewey assails. With that picture there is also associated the belief that any revision of the assumptions on which the procedures of social work rest at any given time can be undertaken only by an elect few who are capable, as the great mass of humanity is not, of carrying out "original research." Against all of these views, Dewey argues that all thinking and all learning is a process of discovery and that as such it involves a testing of the validity of that which is proposed to the learner's mind by the established tradition of social practice. But where there is testing, there is inevitably the possibility of a negative outcome and of a consequent revision of what had previously been accepted as a valid rule of social work. When this model is extended to education as a whole, the familiar claim that it is through the schools and universities that a society renews itself takes on a second and momentous increment of meaning. This renewal will evidently not simply take the form of a training-up of a new generation of replacements for those who currently execute the various social functions to which I have been referring; it also involves a process in which a society submits its prevailing codes of practice to judgment and correction by a succeeding generation—a process of renewal that requires reconstruction rather than simply replacement. As the institutions within which this process of social renewal—conceived in terms of active criticism and reconstruction rather than in terms of passive assimilation—takes place, the schools and universities assume their true social role; and this role is to be as vital a contribution to the life of society as that of any other institution, and certainly not a dim stage of preparation for some eventual participation in the wider social life.

The question that is raised by such a conception as this is not whether its ideal picture of the critical functions which each generation should exercise in relation to the codes of social and scientific practice of prior generations is correct, but rather whether such a picture of the self-revisionary process of human thought at its highest levels provides us with a useful set of metaphors for understanding education as the process by which we reach the point at which we may have something of substance to contribute to such revisions. Doubtless there is much to be said for the inquiry or discovery conception of learning as a technique of instruction; but whatever its merits it would be utterly silly to exaggerate them to the point of obscuring the difference between the kind of "discovery" that reconstructs a process of thought by which some great scientist was led to a fundamental insight and the kind that is literally unprecedented and takes place at the margin of existing knowledge. It also needs to be pointed out that there are areas of study to which even this metaphorical notion of discovery applies much less readily and naturally than it does to others; it is, for example, very hard to see how the study of the French language could be appropriately described in language borrowed from the discovery period.

Finally, although one can agree that it would be

profoundly unfortunate if any form of study went forward without any sense at all of the possibility that it might result in a modification of the body of knowledge that is its object, and that there is thus a continuity, however remote, between all learning and genuine discovery, it will not do to assume as a kind of standard case the very unusual situation in which a difficulty encountered in learning locates a difficulty or incoherency in the corpus of knowledge under study. More generally, it is extremely difficult to develop cogent criticisms or revisions of a body of knowledge or practice while one is still in the process of assimilating it— to be, in other words, at once on the hither and on the far side of a given body of doctrine. If Dewey is right to attack as energetically as he does the passivity of a form of learning that altogether lacks a critical dimension, equally harsh things need to be said about premature efforts to pass over into the critical and reconstructive mode on which Dewey's view sets such a premium and for which in sober fact so few of us are really prepared. For all these reasons it is hard to avoid the conclusion that the business of education is still best described in terms that focus on the process of internalizing the distinctive procedures of a preexistent discipline, including, of course, its own internal criteria of judgment and of criticism, rather than in terms of discovery and reconstruction.

None of the criticisms I have been developing of Dewey's model of inquiry and of the conception of education he based upon it should lead us to underestimate the seriousness of the problem which he hoped to resolve by these means. The simple fact is that education in the sense of continuous organized instruction is typically offered to us at a point in our lives when we are not likely to have asked the questions to which what the school has to offer provides at least some of the answers. In this sense, the discontinuity between our "interests" and the agenda of any serious and sustained form of study is more than just the unfortunate outcome of a badly designed curriculum or of a repressive school environment; it is more plausibly understood as a permanent condition with which schools will always have to contend and which they can minimize but not eliminate. The result is that the opportunity to benefit from education understood as a crash course recapitulating human cultural history for the benefit of latecomers is one which many young people can hardly recognize for what it is and one which they may be unable to profit greatly from because it is not responsive to the interests they in fact have. In our own day it has become common, as it emphatically was not previously, to assume that the reasons for this failure are to be found in the way the schools go about their assigned tasks and also in deeper social evils that block the development of the forms of motivation that are required for a positive response to the opportunity that schooling presents. There is no doubt at all that such failures on the part of the school and the larger society are widespread and serious and that continuing efforts are needed to correct them. But there is a danger that when the commitment to an ideal congruence between interests and the agenda for learning becomes overriding, the school may react to the experience of failure in its effort to connect the interests of its students with substantial academic work by reconstituting itself in such a way as to accommodate its work to these interests as they in fact exist—that is, by redefining its functions in terms of activities in which the great mass of its now universal clientele is capable of participating. Such a policy would quite obviously mark the demise of education understood as the transformation rather than the absolutization of interests; and under such a dispensation the fate of those who desire and can profit from such an education would be predictably grim.

Or so it seems to me. Certainly the main current of liberal opinion in this country has not shared this harsh conclusion, nor have most of the principal philosophers of education who have been the spokesmen for that liberalism. Broadly speaking, their disposition has been to seek a middle ground and to emphasize within the spectrum of the school's activities a number of socially beneficial functions which, it was thought, must have a direct relevance to the lives of all students. In the past, the political temper of this movement was broadly reformist in character and expressed a predominantly positive attitude to the principal institutions of our society through which it hoped to carry out its melioristic aspirations. More recently, a sense of profound alienation from these established institutions and their traditions has been evident and the bland reformist uplift of yesteryear has been replaced by an acrid semi-revolutionary rhetoric. What has remained constant, however, is the disposition to expect of the school and now of the university a continuing exercise of a number of social virtues whose relationship to the special functions and capabilities of the school remains at best problematic. It is this predisposition with its attendant blindness to the identity of the social and the intellectual tasks of the school that constitutes the principal linkage between the older and the more recent phases of what is in many respects a common approach to education. As I have already noted, it has been inspired by the hope that the business of the school might be made palpably relevant to the lives of all its members, and that this could be done by construing the work of the school in terms of activities and interests that spring from the wider life of the society in which all are assumed to share. All too often, however, these generous hopes have issued in programs that achieve this end only by the introduction of a stultifying form of busy-work and the by-passing of those forms of study that enable students to acquire new and more powerful criteria of relevance than their "interests" and their prior social experience can provide them. And at both the secondary and the university level there has been a dismaying tendency to make the thesis of the continuity of interests and inquiry true by fiat through the creation of areas of study that are virtually defined in terms of the interests that generate them rather than in terms of any significant body of knowledge to which the student might address himself.

In referring to the common element in the approaches to education of Dewey and more recent philosophers of education as reflecting a liberal orientation, it is certainly not my intention to endorse the "conservative" approach to education as that is currently understood in this country. Such conservatism has the merit of recognizing that education essentially involves coming up against something that is not just a projection of the interests one already has and that one must work hard to master; but this recognition is associated with a very narrow vision of the scope and implications of such an effort of self-transformation, and it typically finds expression in the kind of vocationalism which is apparently the dominant force in American education today. Perhaps the most unfortunate feature of the American educational scene is the fact that the effective alternatives in matters of educational philosophy are so often confined either to this kind of constricted conservatism or to a liberalism that proclaims the larger interests of the self but proceeds to construe these in such a way as to divorce them from any standard in the light of which they might themselves be judged. I fear that it is a liberalism of this kind which represents for many minds the authoritative interpretation of the democratic principle as it applies to education. In fact, however, it rarely takes even the first steps toward a realistic interpretation of that principle in the light of the actual facts of motivation and ability within the total population and the nature of learning and knowledge as such.

It may be appropriate to close by sketching in another conception of education which does justice, I believe, to its social dimension but in a quite different way from Dewey's. It, too, is a conception of education as initiation of the young into the culture—cognitive, moral and

199

aesthetic—of the society into which they are born, but it recognizes the element of discontinuity that is inevitably present in any such effort to move children within a few years to a position it has taken mankind milennia to reach. It capitalizes on children's predisposing interests to support this effort; but it does not expect any natural congruence between these and the material to be assimilated which is in the first instance, as I have suggested, the established symbolic codes by means of which mankind at its present level does its business. It recognizes that there is much in the cultural legacy of any people to its succeeding generations which can be grasped informally and without any organized effort of instruction; and it also acknowledges that there are those—by no means necessarily unintelligent—for whom the framework of organized instruction will always be uncongenial and who would rather take their chances on such abilities as they may have to catch on to what they need to know. What I am suggesting might be expressed in a metaphor by saying that organized instruction provides at its best a kind of elevator ride to the point which mankind itself has reached by a very hard series of stone steps; and I use this metaphor to convey something of the sudden and precipitate character of the successive acts of abstraction by which we move away from the familiar natural and social terrain of the world in which we begin. It is important to be reminded, as we are repeatedly by Dewey, that the new symbolic apparatus that we learn to use must itself finally serve as an instrument of experiential interpretation and control, and that if it is not to become a sterile and self-sufficient abstraction, we must constantly ask ourselves how a given concept is to be applied and used in the differential contexts of experience.

Nevertheless, the fact remains that the process of mastering, of internalizing a preexistent idiom of thought is very different in respect of the kind of communication and sociality it entails from the form of experience that precedes such a process. I would want to argue, indeed, that this process is distinctive in a way that makes efforts to understand it in terms of metaphors drawn from the sphere of cooperative social work either un-helpful because the model of sociality used is too crude, or circular because it already incorporates the distinc-tive features it was intended to explain. Beyond that I would suggest that if a case for such distinctiveness can be made along lines like those proposed in this paper, there will also be reason to think that the social func-tion of the school and the university—the institutions within which processes of this kind are to take place—must be allowed its own kind of distinctiveness, and that homogenizing analogies drawn from a broader domain of social processes are out of place in serious efforts to characterize the kind of society that schools are to be.[1]

Note

1. The account which I have given here of Dewey's theory of inquiry is based upon such works as *Human Nature and Conduct, Experience and Nature*, and *The Quest for Certainty;* and my account of his educational philosophy derives principally from *Democracy and Education*. I have, however, given careful attention to Dewey's later *Experience and Education*, which many regard as an important statement of dissent from the more extreme kind of progressivism. There can be no doubt that in that book Dewey does express reservations as to some aspects of the kind of educational practice that had claimed the authority of his philosophy of education; but one could also wish that he had been more willing to acknowledge a measure of responsibility for these excesses if only by reason of the vague and unguarded character of some of his own earlier pronouncements. In the matter of the relationship between experience and inquiry on which the central theses of his philosophy of education rest and with which this essay concerns itself, I am unable to see that *Experience and Education* deviates in any significant way from Dewey's earlier position. It is true that in this book he recognizes the distinction between the "objective" conditions for learning and the "internal" or psychological conditions; and he declares that progressive education must not simply reverse the procedure of "traditional education" and subordinate the objective conditions one-sidedly to the "internal" conditions. But the significance of such a corrective observation is considerably diminished by Dewey's continuing polemic against the view that the knowledge that is to be imparted is "pre-existent" and by his claim that "intellectual organization is not an end in itself but is a means by which social relations, distinctively human ties and bonds, may be understood and more intelligently ordered" (1938; reprinted New York, Collier Books, 1963, p. 83). Observations like this express precisely the kind of confusion between different forms of "social life" which I criticize in this essay. Similar ambiguities seem to me to characterize the notion of experience that is invoked in *Experience and Education;* and if Dewey is slightly more willing than he was earlier to acknowledge the directive role of the teacher and thus of the accumulated adult "experience" which

the teacher represents, "imposition" remains as before under a severe interdict and it still "goes without saying that the organized subject-matter of the adult and the specialist cannot provide the starting point" (p. 82). But if the special positions of the teacher and the "objective conditions' of education are to mean anything, then that "organized subject-matter" *must* be the starting point for the design of a curriculum. Otherwise, we will be left as before with the forlorn hope that the "experiences" of students will be of such a character as to lead them "from a social and human center to a more objective intellectual scheme of organization" (p. 83).

Index

205

Index

Index

Index

Index

Index

Rules, in art, 106–111, 116
Rundle, Bede, 147
Russell, Bertrand, 22, 25, 30, 31, 50, 51, 126–127, 145, 146; *Roads to Freedom*, 6
Ryle, Gilbert, 66

Santayana, George, 19, 23, 43, 44, 46–47, 53, 56, 60, 72; *Reason in Society*, 19
Sartre, Jean-Paul, 7, 70
Schilpp, Paul Arthur, 72, 145, 146, 147, 148
Schools: Dewey's view of role in society of, 10; his advice to, 24; his contribution to, 26–29; and society, relationship between, 174–178; basic problem faced by, 195–197; response of, to the problem, 197–198. *See also* Education; Teachers
Science, 125; contribution of Dewey's views on, 14–16; and democracy, 16–21, 23; and politics, 20–21; and morals and art, 70; as exemplar, 75; practice of, similar to art?, 103–104; what it does, according to Dewey, 141; his positive view of, 173–174; natural, *see* Natural science. *See also* Scientific method
Scientific method: belief in, urged by Dewey, 9 ff.; unsatisfactory response to need for, 12–13; Dewey's application to metaphysics, 47, 49; in philosophy, 58. *See also* Science

Self-consciousness, 55–58
Sellars, Wilfrid, 50, 65, 66, 73, 141–142, 143, 144, 147
Sensations, 63
Sentences, 119–122, 124, 126; ethical, 155–158, 160–161. *See also* Language
Shaw, George Bernard, 30, 31
"Situations," in Dewey's philosophy, 138–144
Skinner, B. F., 145
Snow, C. P., 70
Social philosophy, Dewey's, 3–44; his social positions undefined, 6–8, 12; distinctive manner of dealing with issues, 9–10, 30–35, 37; recurrent doctrines, 9–10; science and democracy, 16–26; the public, 35–37; people in conflict, 38; summary, 39–43
Social programs, problems of, 11–12
Social sciences, 52; poor record of, 10; possible new view, 70
Socialism, 7
Society, and school, interrelationship between, 174–178
Socrates (Socratic), 42
Spencer, Herbert, 7, 18
Spinoza, Baruch, 59; *Ethics*, 45; *Political Treatise*, 44
Statement, artistic, 91; contrasted with expression, 81
Stevenson, Charles L., 153, 155–156, 163, 164, 170, 171
Suppes, Patrick, 146

Taylor, Charles, 145